JUL 2005

# JIMMY CARTER

PRESIDENTIAL ✦ LEADERS

# JIMMY CARTER

## BEVERLY GHERMAN

LERNER PUBLICATIONS COMPANY/MINNEAPOLIS

For my son Greg, to share with his sons

Racial terms change over time. In the 1930s and 1940s, when Jimmy Carter was growing up, he referred to his friends and neighbors as blacks. Earlier, his parents' generation had called them coloreds or Negroes. In the 1990s, African American had become a more accepted usage. Terms used in the text reflect the times.

Lerner Publications Company
A division of Lerner Publishing Group
241 First Avenue North
Minneapolis, MN 55401 U.S.A.

Website address: www.lernerbooks.com

Library of Congress Cataloging-in-Publication Data

Gherman, Beverly
    Jimmy Carter / by Beverly Gherman.
       p.   cm. — (Presidential leaders)
    Includes bibliographical references and index.
    Summary: Profiles former peanut farmer, Georgia governor, and United States president Jimmy Carter, including his ongoing promotion of social justice and human rights around the world.
    ISBN: 0–8225–0816–8 (lib. bdg. : alk. paper)
    1. Carter, Jimmy, 1924– —Juvenile literature.  2. Presidents—United States—Biography—Juvenile literature. [1. Carter, Jimmy, 1924–  2. Presidents.] I. Title. II. Series.
E873.G48  2004
973.926'092—dc21                                                                        2003003558

Manufactured in the United States of America
1 2 3 4 5 6 – JR – 09 08 07 06 05 04

# CONTENTS

———— ✧ ————

*Jimmy carter holds up his Nobel Peace Prize.*

# INTRODUCTION

*At the beginning of this new Millennium
I was asked to discuss, here in Oslo, the
greatest challenge that the world faces.
Among all the possible choices, I decided
that the most serious and universal problem
is the growing chasm [gap] between the
richest and poorest people on earth.*

—Jimmy Carter, accepting his
Nobel Peace Prize in 2002

At 4 A.M. on Friday morning, October 11, 2002, former president Jimmy Carter was awakened by a phone call. The head of the Nobel Peace Prize Committee, Gunnar Berge, was calling to tell him he had been chosen to receive the Nobel Peace Prize. At first, "I thought it was a joke," he later told reporters. But Berge convinced him that the award was real. It was being given "for his decades of untiring effort to find peaceful solutions to international conflicts, to advance democracy and human rights and to promote economic and social development."

The committee said his great skill was in preventing conflicts. In 1994, when U.S. warships were heading toward the tiny Caribbean nation of Haiti, Carter "averted a bloody crisis by persuading the military junta [rulers] to leave." That same year, he traveled to the Asian country of North Korea to settle disputes over nuclear weapons in that country. A year later, he helped resolve problems between two African nations, Sudan and Uganda. He is used to receiving phone calls during the night asking him to help in one country or another. That's what he expected when the phone rang this time.

Later that Friday, the six hundred people of Plains, Georgia, Carter's hometown, came together to celebrate with Carter. A *New York Times* reporter wrote, "There were farmers in straw hats, fanning themselves with Nobel Peace programs, teachers and students, clerks from the local shops." Everyone was hugging and cheering and waving banners with Jimmy Carter's name imprinted on them.

On the evening news, TV anchor Peter Jennings described Jimmy Carter's latest award as a "stepping-stone to greatness." Beginning in his presidency in the 1970s, when he worked tirelessly to create a peace treaty between the two warring countries of Israel and Egypt, Carter has always believed in solving disputes through dialogue and diplomacy. In 2002 the Nobel committee acknowledged and rewarded his many years of waging peace.

Each year the Norwegian Nobel committee receives nominations for the prize. Carter had been suggested many times in the past, and when he won that year, many felt it was about time. The Nobel Peace Prize had been given to Egypt's Anwar al-Sadat and Israel's Menachem Begin after

Carter's persuasive diplomacy led them to sign a peace treaty in 1978. The committee explained that Carter's nomination had not been received before the deadline then, and, therefore, it could not be considered.

U.S. journalist Molly Ivins wrote that his award was "recognition of how long and how hard Jimmy Carter has worked for peace and human rights. I think he is an invaluable asset to the nation."

Carter, his wife Rosalynn, and their family and friends traveled to Oslo, Norway, a few days before the December ceremony. On the afternoon of December 10, 2002, Carter met with the queen of Norway. With a fanfare of trumpets, he was escorted into the elegant auditorium of Oslo City Hall. He received his medal and a hand-lettered certificate from the chairman of the Norwegian Nobel committee.

With the award came a check for one million dollars. Carter said he would accept the Nobel cash award on behalf of "suffering people around the world." He would give the money to the Carter Center, which he had established in Atlanta, the capital of Georgia, where it would be used as an emergency fund for preventing future conflicts.

Jimmy Carter made no attempt to hide his pleasure at receiving the Nobel Peace Prize. In his speech, he explained, "I am not here as a public official, but as a citizen of a troubled world," who urges countries to find peaceful ways to coexist. He ended by saying:

> War may sometimes be a necessary evil. But no matter how necessary, it is always evil, never a good. We will not learn how to live together in peace by killing each other's children.

# THE NOBEL PEACE PRIZE

Alfred Nobel was born in Stockholm, Sweden, in October 1833 and died in 1896. He developed the processes for making nitroglycerin and dynamite. These and many other chemical and engineering discoveries made him a wealthy man. Because he always regretted that his own work on dynamite was used for warfare, he stated in his will that his fortune be used to establish a fund to reward individuals whose contributions benefited mankind. The Nobel Prize Committee gives awards in medicine, physics and chemistry, economics, literature—which are chosen in Sweden—and a separate prize for peace. The Norwegian Congress selects the five-person committee to choose the winner of the peace prize from those who have been nominated.

The Nobel Peace Prize is presented in the Oslo City Hall. The other medals are presented in the Concert Hall in Stockholm, Sweden. All of them are awarded on December 10, the anniversary of Nobel's death.

The chairperson of the Norwegian Nobel Committee hands the recipient of the peace prize a velvet-lined box containing the gold medal. On one side of the medal is the head of Alfred Nobel *(right)*. On the reverse side are three male figures with arms joined. The inscription in Latin reads: *pro pace et fraternitate gentium,* meaning "for the peace and brotherhood of men." The winner's name is engraved on the medal.

*Carter and his wife, Rosalynn* (front right), *attend a concert in December 2002, during the Nobel Peace Prize ceremonies in Oslo, Norway.*

─────────── ✧ ───────────

That evening the Carters attended a banquet in the same ornate building where he had received his award. The Nobel Peace Prize may have been twenty-four years late in coming but was even more meaningful for its recognition of all Jimmy Carter had accomplished for world peace in those intervening years.

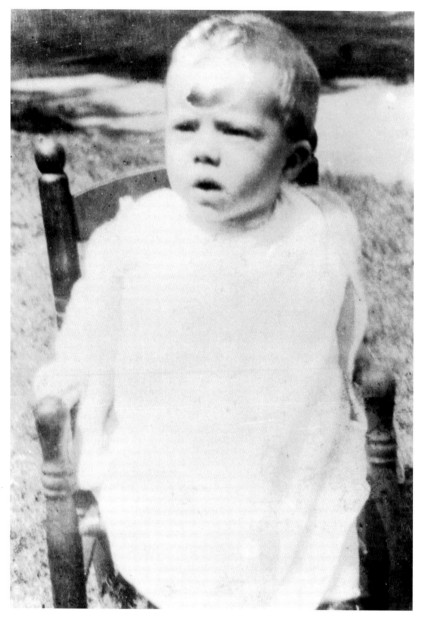

*One-year-old Jimmy sits for a photograph.*

CHAPTER ONE

# ON THE FARM

*My life on the farm during the Great
Depression more nearly resembled farm life of
fully 2,000 years ago than farm life today.*
—Jimmy Carter

Jimmy Carter was born on October 1, 1924, in the Wise
Clinic in Plains, Georgia. He was the first U.S. president to
be born in a hospital. Earlier presidents had been born at
home.

Jimmy grew up in the tiny town of Archery, on his
daddy's farm. As a boy, he delighted in how the red clay
dirt felt on his bare feet. He loved the land just as his
daddy, Earl Carter, did. Earl owned hundreds of acres of
land on which he grew cotton and peanuts. He also owned
a warehouse where he processed the crops. He employed
black field hands to help him plant and harvest. The workers lived in small clapboard houses around the property,
and their children were Jimmy's friends.

*Miss Lillian Carter holds her son Jimmy on her lap.*
✧ ————————

His mother, Lillian, known as Miss Lillian by the townspeople, worked as a nurse at the Wise Clinic hospital. She raised her family with the help of the black women who lived nearby. After Jimmy was born, the Carters had two daughters—Gloria in 1926 and Ruth in 1929—and then thirteen years later, in 1937, another son, Billy, was born.

Jimmy stayed with Rachel and Jack Clark, a black family, when his parents went out of town, and he felt "most at home" there. They had a small house, and Jimmy slept on the floor on a pallet stuffed with straw.

Rachel Clark took him fishing. She taught him about nature and how to behave. Jack Clark was his daddy's farm manager. Jack taught him how to use tools, how to plant, and how to harvest the cotton and peanuts they grew on the farm.

By 1930 the country was going through a period of economic hardship called the Great Depression. Jobs were scarce. Many men rode trains from town to town looking for work. People called these people hoboes or tramps. They often knocked at the Carters' back door asking for a meal. Jimmy's mother always found something to share with them. She wondered why so many of these men stopped at her house. The mystery was solved sometime later when she found marks on her mailbox post made by one of the tramps and learned that the marks were a code, telling other travelers she wouldn't turn them away.

## HARD WORK

Earl was a tough taskmaster. He expected Jimmy to work hard and to do things right. Every Sunday morning, he

————————————— ✧
From left to right: Gloria, Ruth, and Jimmy pose with their father outside their farmhouse in Archery, Georgia.

gave Jimmy a penny to put in the collection plate at Sunday school. One Sunday afternoon, Earl found two pennies on Jimmy's dresser. That meant Jimmy had taken a penny out of the plate, rather than putting one in. Jimmy received a whipping that he never forgot, and he never stole anything again.

From the age of five, Jimmy worked as hard as his parents did. One of his first jobs was to sell boiled peanuts in Plains. He took his wagon into the fields, filled it with peanut vines, and pulled it home again. He picked off the peanuts, washed the dirt from them, and soaked them overnight in salty water. Then they had to be boiled for about thirty minutes. Once they were dry, he filled small paper sacks with the peanuts. He packed the sacks into a basket so that he could sell them in town. When he was older, he rode his bike into Plains and managed to make as much as one dollar when he sold all his sacks.

Miss Lillian was an avid reader. She encouraged Jimmy and his siblings to read and even suggested that they bring their books to the table. They read during meals except for Sunday dinner. Earl didn't share their love of books, but he read newspapers and kept up with local politics.

Jimmy tried to model himself after his daddy. He hunted and fished with Earl and worked as hard as he could to please him. After their midday dinner, when Earl stretched out for a rest on the floor of the front porch, Jimmy "relished lying beside him."

When Jimmy was eleven, Earl installed a windmill to provide running water for the kitchen and bathroom. That meant the Carters would have indoor plumbing and would

*Jimmy loved life on the farm.*

———————— ◇ ————————

no longer have to go to the outdoor privy. Before that, the family used the outhouse twenty yards from the back door. They saved old newspapers or pages from the Sears Roebuck catalog to use as toilet paper.

The Carter family used kerosene lamps for lighting and had a battery-powered radio so that they could hear their favorite programs, such as *Fibber McGee and Molly, Jack Benny,* and *Little Orphan Annie.* By 1938 electricity had come to the area. The Carters had electric lighting installed throughout the house to replace the kerosene lamps. A refrigerator replaced the old-fashioned icebox, and a new electric stove replaced the old wood-burning one.

## FRIENDSHIPS

Growing up on the farm, Jimmy's best friends were black—the children of the tenant farmers who worked for his father. The three friends, Jimmy, A. D., and Edmund, never thought about the differences among them. It didn't matter to them that Jimmy was white and they were black. Or that his daddy owned the "big house," and they lived in tenant shacks. They were friends who played together, fished together, explored the fields and creek banks together.

From March to October, the boys went barefoot despite the hot earth, rough tree bark, and splintery floors. By the time they were thirteen, they were expected to wear shoes to church and school.

*Jimmy* (top left), *Gloria* (bottom left), *and Ruth*
(bottom right) *sit with friends*

Sometimes Jimmy and A. D. took the train to Americus, thirteen miles away, to see a movie at the Rylander Theater. They walked to the railroad stop, and they waved for the train to pick them up. On the train, they each paid fifteen cents to the conductor. A. D. sat in what was called the "colored" section, Jimmy in the "white" section. Once they reached Americus, they walked together until they reached the theater. Jimmy went to the front entrance, paid ten cents to see the movie, and sat down-stairs. A. D. went to the back entrance, paid his dime, and climbed to the third level. They split up again when they took the train home. They thought their day in Americus was wonderful. And neither of them questioned why they had to separate so much.

As an adult looking back, Jimmy said most people then gave little thought to the segregation between black and white families. It was "accepted like breathing."

But one day, things changed between Jimmy and his friends. By then Jimmy, A. D., and Edmund were teenagers. The three of them were walking from the barn toward the pasture. When they reached a gate, A. D. and Edmund opened it and "stepped back to let [Jimmy] go through first." That had never happened before. Jimmy thought they had cooked up some sort of trick for him. Maybe they had a wire across the opening or a trap on the ground.

Finally, he got up his courage to walk through the gate. Nothing happened. Then he realized that his friends were suddenly aware of the differences among them. Maybe their parents had said something. But no matter what the reason, it was a change. "[A] precious sense of equality had gone out of our personal relationship, and things were never again the same between them and me," Jimmy said later.

## HIGH SCHOOL

Once Jimmy was in high school, there were many changes in his life. He began making new friends at his all-white school, because his black friends had gone to an all-black high school. He was not selling peanuts any longer, but he was still eager to earn money. He and his cousin Hugh sold homemade ice cream and hamburgers on Saturdays at a downtown stand. Plains was crowded with families doing their shopping and errands, and the boys usually sold all their ice cream, three dips for five cents, and hamburger sandwiches, for another five cents. Jimmy also worked in his Uncle Buddy's store on Saturday nights and whenever he was needed to help take inventory.

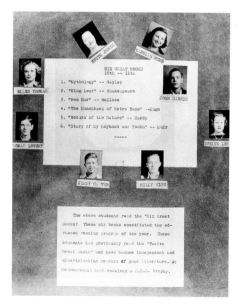

During the last two years of high school, Jimmy played varsity basketball. He was the smallest player on the team, and the others called him "Peewee," but he was fast. He was also the biggest reader. One year, he won the contest for reading the most books at Plains High School. His teacher gave

✧ ———————————

*Jimmy was among eight students to read six great English-language novels at Plains High School.*

*Jimmy (first row, far right) graduated from Plains High School in 1941.*

———————— ✧ ————————

him a reproduction of a famous painting, *The Blue Boy* by the English artist Thomas Gainsborough, which he hung on his bedroom wall.

In 1941 Jimmy graduated from Plains High School. There were twenty-six students in his class, and he was the only one to continue his education. He should have been the valedictorian of his class, the one with the highest grades, who would deliver the graduation speech. But he had skipped school on senior day, and he was punished by having his grades lowered. This lowered his overall grade average. Jimmy said it was a great relief not to have to stand up in front of his classmates to deliver a speech. As comfortable as he was at home and had been on the farm with his black friends, he was still not at ease with his Plains High School classmates.

## CHAPTER TWO

# FUTURE DREAMS

*I don't know how to compromise on any
principle I believe is right.*

—Jimmy Carter

Jimmy's uncle, Tom Watson Gordy, had joined the navy in the late 1920s when he was seventeen. He had sent Jimmy letters and photographs from all the exotic ports he visited. Life on a ship seemed thrilling to Jimmy, and he decided he would go into the navy, too, and visit the same ports his uncle had described. In the meantime, he treasured a photograph that showed Uncle Tom holding a trophy for winning the boxing championship of the Pacific Fleet.

A few years later, he told his parents he planned eventually to go to Annapolis, Maryland, the location of the U.S. Naval Academy, to become a naval officer. To show them he was serious, he wrote to the Naval Academy asking for information about its requirements. But he didn't mention in the letter that he was only in grade school.

Jimmy discovered that physical requirements were as important as good grades. The academy said that applicants needed to have straight teeth, and he worried that his teeth did not exactly meet. Applicants needed to reach a certain height and weight. He worried that he would never grow tall enough or heavy enough.

As he grew older, he learned that a young man also needed support from his senator or congressman to be appointed to the academy. His father stayed in close touch with Congressman Stephen Pace of Georgia, hoping that he would support Jimmy's appointment to the Naval Academy.

Unfortunately, when Jimmy graduated from high school in 1941, Congressman Pace had already chosen his candidate for the coming year. Jimmy was disappointed, but he wasn't going to give up. In the meantime, he enrolled at the two-year Georgia Southwestern College in Americus.

When the Japanese attacked the U.S. military base in Pearl Harbor in the Hawaiian Islands in December 1941, the United States entered World War II (1939–1945). Jimmy was even more certain about what he wanted to do. He told his college friends that after Annapolis, he intended to become a submarine commander in the United States Navy. None of his family had finished high school, let alone attended university or the illustrious Naval Academy. His mother had always wanted a college education, but instead she took nurse's training at the Wise Clinic in Plains. Jimmy thought that his chances for receiving an appointment to the Naval Academy were slim.

In the summer of 1942, Congressman Pace recommended Jimmy for an appointment to the academy to begin the following year. The academy told him that he

*This photo of Jimmy was taken in 1942 before he enrolled at the Naval Academy.*

———— ✧ ————

would be required to take more science classes than Southwestern offered, so he decided to attend Georgia Tech in Atlanta. This large university was a new challenge. Jimmy took engineering courses in navigation, seamanship, and military science, and he joined the naval ROTC (Reserve Officers Training Corps) to learn how to be a navy officer.

While at Georgia Tech, he learned more than science. His roommate loved classical music and played his phonograph records all the time, which exposed Jimmy to famous composers. Listening to Wagner's opera *Tristan and Isolde* or Beethoven's symphonies became a lifetime pleasure for him.

In Atlanta he was exposed to life in a big city too. It was very different from the life he was used to in small-town Plains. At first, he felt more comfortable spending his weekends at home, but he began staying at school so he could attend football games and root for Georgia Tech.

## ANNAPOLIS

At last, it was time for him to attend the Naval Academy. When he was almost nineteen, in June 1943, Jimmy took a train to Washington, D.C., and then a bus to the Academy in nearby Maryland on Chesapeake Bay. He passed his physical, weighing in at 121 pounds, which was just heavy enough to meet the requirement. Apparently, his height and his teeth were acceptable as well.

Everything about life at the academy was difficult. The first-year students were called plebes and were taunted by upperclassmen. They were made to sing or do push-ups or eat in strange ways as a form of hazing. If they didn't follow orders, upperclassmen paddled them with brooms. Jimmy wrote in his diary about how sore his bottom was, but he was used to his father's strict discipline at home and on the farm. He knew he could get through the first year. Every Monday morning while at the academy, Jimmy rose early to say the academy motto, "Another week in which to excel!" It fit in with his own high standards to do well.

The summer after that first year in Annapolis, Jimmy moved from the classroom to an actual ship to gain experience in operating and maintaining the vessel. He was also expected to fire an antiaircraft gun during regular practice alerts.

## PARTNER FOR LIFE

Rosalynn Smith, a close friend of Jimmy's sister Ruth had fallen in love with Jimmy's picture pinned up on Ruth's bedroom wall. He was the glamorous older man she had known since she was a girl. She remembered buying ice cream from Jimmy's stand in Plains and had admired him even then.

When Jimmy came home on leave from the Naval Academy during the summer of 1945, Ruth invited Rosalynn to help them clean up the Pond House, which Earl had built a few miles from town near a lake. Jimmy teased Rosalynn a lot that day as they worked on the grounds and inside the house. When he invited her to go to a movie that evening, she accepted.

Rosalynn remembers, "I was completely swept off my feet" by Jimmy. That night Jimmy told his mother how much he had enjoyed being with Rosalynn. "She's the girl I want to marry," he said.

Jimmy had to return to Annapolis two days after their date. When Rosalynn came to the train station to say good-bye, Jimmy asked her to write to him. He wasn't concerned that Rosalynn, seventeen, was too young for him.

*Rosalynn Smith was smitten with Jimmy.*

——————— ✧ ———————

From Annapolis Jimmy and his classmates immediately left on a ship bound for the North Atlantic. The United States had been fighting World War II against Germany and Japan since 1941. Although a peace agreement had been signed with Germany in early May, 1945, the war with Japan was still ongoing. The young men were certain they were heading for the invasion of Japan. This was wartime, not one of Uncle Tom's peacetime visits to a colorful port.

After they had been sailing just a few days, they were ordered on deck for important news. Over the ship's loudspeakers, they heard President Truman make the startling announcement that a "superbomb had just been dropped on Japan." It was August 6, 1945. Three days later, a second atomic bomb was dropped on another Japanese city, and Japan surrendered shortly afterward. World War II was over! Jimmy's ship immediately returned to port.

Rosalynn wrote him that the people of Plains had gone to church to give thanks for peace. At the time, no one realized the horror of the bombings—how atomic bombs would kill or disfigure at least 270,000 Japanese people. President Truman justified his decision to drop the bombs by saying their use would end the war and prevent thousands of young Japanese and U.S. men from being killed.

Jimmy and Rosalynn continued to write to each other while he was in Annapolis. At Christmastime Jimmy came home on leave. At last, he and Rosalynn could be together and get to know one another. They went to parties and movies. Just before he had to return to Annapolis, Jimmy asked her to marry him. Rosalynn said no.

───────────── ✧
*Jimmy signed his portait to Rosalynn, "Darling, I love you with all my heart—for all my life. —Jimmy."*

*Rosalynn* (left) *and Lillian* (right) *pin on Jimmy's naval bars upon his graduation from the Naval Academy at Annapolis.*

There was no question that Rosalynn loved Jimmy and wanted to be with him. But when she was thirteen, she had promised her dying father she would go to college. He had not had that opportunity, and he wanted all four of his children to get a good education. When Jimmy asked Rosalynn to marry him, she was enrolled in nearby Georgia Southwestern College in Americus.

After Jimmy returned to the academy, they wrote each other every day. He invited Rosalynn to come with his parents for a visit in February. He proposed again. Rosalynn said yes this time, but they decided to keep it secret.

In June 1946, Jimmy graduated from the Naval Academy. Rosalynn returned with his parents for the graduation ceremony. When he received his commission as an ensign (the lowest officer's rank in the navy) and his naval bars, Rosalynn pinned them on one shoulder of his uniform. His mother pinned them on the other shoulder. He had done well, graduating with nearly a 3.5 grade average out of a possible 4.0.

He had learned to handle weapons and to identify all types of ships and planes. He was a cross-country runner on the track team, played football with the lightweight team, and became adept at sailing small boats. He also decided it would be valuable to take ballroom dancing lessons and public-speaking lessons so that he would be more well-rounded socially.

*Happy and in love, Carter and Rosalynn were married shortly after Carter graduated from the academy.*

# CHAPTER THREE

# A NEW LIFE

*I don't worry about the prospects of future disappointments or embarrassments or difficulties. I take one thing at a time, do the best I can, and then if I fail, I don't dwell on it or bemoan it. I just go on.*

—Jimmy Carter

Just a month after graduation, Carter and Rosalynn were married in the Methodist church in Plains before their families and a small group of friends. As punctual as Carter always was, he was almost late for the wedding because he hadn't allowed enough time to pick up Rosalynn at her home and drive to the church.

## IN THE NAVY

The newlyweds began their married life in Norfolk, Virginia. All naval assignments were chosen by lottery, so Carter couldn't complain when he was assigned to the USS

*Carter* (front row, third from left) *with some of the crew of the USS* Wyoming

*Wyoming,* an old battleship that was going to test new navigation radar. Carter's duty kept him at sea from Monday to Thursday, and he was required to be on duty every third night too, including weekends.

Rosalynn was alone a great deal. Their apartment was pleasant, but she was lonely. She had left all her friends and family in Plains and didn't know a soul in Norfolk. But she managed to take care of all their bills on the $300 monthly salary Carter received. (In today's money that salary would equal almost $3,000.) Since little money was left for going out, they bought a record player to listen to the records Carter had won from his roommate in a coin toss.

### FIRST SON
The Carters' first child was born on July 3, 1947. They named him John William Carter and called him Jack.

Carter was able to stay home for two weeks to help Rosalynn with the baby. She did well until he had to go back to work. Then she found it difficult to manage. Even getting food into the house was a major problem because she had a long trip by streetcar, carrying the baby, then the long return trip carrying her groceries and the baby as well.

As sad and homesick as Rosalynn felt, she learned not to cry. "Carter had and still has no patience with tears," she wrote. He expected her to do her best and to do it with a smile, because that was the way he approached everything.

## SUBMARINE SCHOOL

In June 1948, Carter was chosen for a six-month assignment to submarine officer training school in New London, Connecticut, with sixty other junior officers. They all lived in apartments on the submarine base, and he was home every evening. A couple living nearby was from Peru, and Carter and Rosalynn studied Spanish with them.

At school Carter worked hard learning facts in the classroom and practical skills on a submarine. The submarine course was

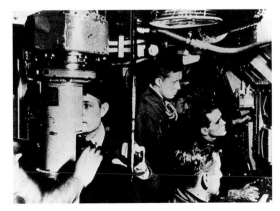

*Carter* (standing center) *worked hard in submarine training school.*

intensive, but he did well, standing third in the class of fifty-two. He was then assigned to serve as an electronics officer on the USS *Pomfret* based in Honolulu, Hawaii.

He and Rosalynn were thrilled about the assignment. First, they drove to Plains for Christmas in their new car. While Rosalynn and baby Jack stayed with her mother, Carter left for a three-month cruise to China on his new submarine. He kept to himself on the ship. Instead of joining the others for poker after dinner, he went back to his bunk to read or study.

One night as he stood watch, he was swept off the bridge by an enormous wave. He was able to swim in the roiling waters until he was swept back onto the submarine at almost the same spot where he had been standing before. Carter learned that it was one of the worst storms ever recorded in the Pacific Ocean, and he knew how lucky he had been. The sub lost its radio and could not make the normal daily report that all hands were safe. Naval headquarters assumed the ship had sunk. Luckily, Rosalynn was still in Plains, unaware that there had been any danger, until after it had passed.

## HAWAII

The ship returned to Hawaii in March 1949, and Carter found an apartment in Honolulu, so Rosalynn and the baby could join him. They quickly settled in. Carter even had time to learn woodworking in the navy shops, when he wasn't studying for his submarine exams. He passed the exams in February 1950, and this time, Rosalynn pinned on his dolphins (the submarine emblem that includes two dolphins). The emblem signified that he was qualified to serve on a submarine and that he was familiar with every valve and switch the sub contained.

A few months later, on April 12, 1950, the Carters' second son was born. They named him James Earl Carter III and called him Chip from the beginning.

The Carters soon had to give up the idyllic life in Honolulu, with its mild temperature and beautiful scenery. The Korean War began in 1950, and Carter's submarine was sent to San Diego, California. Rosalynn and the boys joined him there. Housing was scarce, because many servicemen were stationed in San Diego before they went to Korea. Carter found an apartment for the family in a poor neighborhood, where they were able to use their Spanish language skills with the neighbors.

## SUBMARINE DUTY

After five months, the four of them returned to Connecticut. Carter was to be the engineering officer on a new submarine, called *K-1*. His crewmates called him "Jim" and found him "professional, organized, smart as hell," but still, he kept his distance and didn't make close friends with the other men. He left their social relationships up to Rosalynn.

A third son, Donnel Jeffrey, was born on August 18, 1952. They called him Jeff. Meanwhile, Carter found time to work on furniture-making projects. One was a cabinet for their record player. Together, he and Rosalynn went fishing, and they watched baseball games on their first television set. Living in the eastern United States meant they had snowstorms, which they hadn't experienced in Georgia. They loved the snow and took the boys sledding.

Carter wrote a research paper to qualify as a submarine commander. His paper dealt with passive listening devices for underwater use. The system he developed helped to determine the distance to other ships in the area. This was especially important for tracking enemy vessels. Still ambitious to move up in rank, Carter applied for an advanced nuclear submarine program headed by Captain Hyman Rickover in Schenectady, New York.

*Captain Hyman Rickover* (shown here as an admiral) *had a profound effect on Carter's life.*

———— ✧ ————

During a grueling two-hour interview, Rickover asked him how he had done at Annapolis. "Sir, I stood fifty-ninth in my class of 820!" Carter answered with pride. But then, instead of congratulating him, Rickover asked another question. "Did you do your best?" Carter hesitated. He wanted to say yes, but he knew that wasn't the truth. "No sir, I didn't *always* do my best."

Carter was accepted into the program, but Rickover's question had become a challenge for him. He knew that in the future he would always have to do his best.

CHAPTER FOUR

# RETURN TO PLAINS

*I had only one life to live, and I wanted to live it as a civilian, with a potentially fuller opportunity for varied public service.*

—Jimmy Carter

Early in 1953, Carter's mother called to tell him that Earl was dying of pancreatic cancer. He drove to Georgia to spend time with his daddy. Carter had always thought of Earl as a disciplinarian who worked hard and expected everyone around him to do the same. But while he was home, he saw a different person. "His accomplishments and the breadth of his interests were astonishing to me," Carter recalled. He also saw how the people of Plains respected Earl. Visitors came all day long, bringing him treats or checking to see how he was feeling. Earl had worked in the community his whole life. He had helped families in need without telling anyone, and he had just been elected to the state legislature. He had made a difference in his hometown.

After his father's death, Carter drove back to his family in Schenectady, New York. On the long drive, he began to question his own life and the decisions he had made. He was successful in his naval career and believed he would continue to rise in the ranks. As he considered his father's life, though, he realized a naval career would never compare to what his daddy had done for the community as a scientific farmer and as a state legislator. Becoming chief engineer of a nuclear submarine would be fulfilling, but he wanted his life to have more meaning. He decided to give up his naval career and return to Plains, where he would help his mother by running the farm.

He greeted Rosalynn with his decision. She was shocked. She liked the independence she had gained away from her mother and her mother-in-law. She liked the new friends she had made and the opportunity to travel and live in many different locations. She pleaded with him to change his mind, but she also knew that he would not budge.

Once they were back in Plains, they moved into a small apartment in subsidized public housing. It was all they could afford. By then Jack was in first grade, Chip was three, and Jeff was one. The Carter land holdings were extensive, but the cotton and peanut crops had failed for several years because of a lengthy drought. Carter had to take out a large loan from the bank to keep the farm going. He started taking agricultural classes to learn up-to-date scientific methods to improve production. He had been away from farming for eleven years, and much had changed. He studied how to grow better corn, cotton, and peanuts. He learned how to keep accurate records, how to build and mend fences, and how to treat stored grain to keep it fresh.

*After his father's death, Carter and Rosalynn returned to Plains, Georgia (above), to run the family's peanut farm.*

──────── ✧ ────────

## FITTING IN

By 1955 conditions had improved. The droughts were over. It rained frequently, and the crops grew well. Customers were able to pay their bills, and they had enormous quantities of peanuts to process in the Carter warehouse. The family was finally able to leave public housing and could afford to rent a house with more space inside and out.

Rosalynn went to the warehouse to keep the account books, taking the younger boys with her. She found that she really enjoyed getting out of the house and that she was good at balancing the books.

Soon Carter had time to work in the community. He became a member of the local country club and joined the

Lions Club—a group that funded local projects. One of the Lions' first projects was to pave the rough dirt streets in Plains. Before long, the club had built a swimming pool for the town, although it was restricted to whites only.

On May 17, 1954, the U.S. Supreme Court had decided *Brown v. Board of Education.* The Court had declared that segregation in the public schools was unconstitutional. Carter knew that this decision would be difficult for Plains, because the schools there always had been segregated. Soon a group called the White Citizens Council was formed to fight the Supreme Court decision. The leaders expected Carter to join with them. They came to visit him and to collect five dollars as dues. Carter said he would not join, that he "would as soon flush five dollars down the toilet." The men threatened to cause trouble for his business, but he was adamant.

After that, several customers pulled out of his warehouse, and he and Rosalynn had to pump their own gas at the filling station, unheard of in those years. The family's membership at the country club was abruptly ended too. Rosalynn found this out when she dropped Chip off for his golf lesson, and he was turned away.

Carter didn't want to harm his business by openly fighting for the Supreme Court decision, but he knew it was time to change the policy of separate schools for black and white students. He had lived with segregation his whole life and accepted it, but not anymore.

Carter joined the school board in 1956 and later became its chairman. He was also a Boy Scout leader, while Rosalynn served as den mother for the boys' Cub Scout troop. Carter also assisted in the search for a doctor to move to the area, and he saw to it that a modern medical clinic was built.

# School Segregation

From the beginning of U.S. history, black students were not allowed to attend schools with white students. In 1896 a case heard by the Supreme Court, *Plessy v. Ferguson*, upheld the doctrine of separate but equal schools for African Americans, although the schools' facilities and supplies were not equal.

In 1954 *Brown v. Board of Education* overturned the earlier decision, stating that it violated the Fourteenth Amendment. This amendment, approved in 1868, guaranteed equal protection under the law. Because of *Brown*, schools would need to desegregage (no longer be separated by race).

Individual states did not always comply immediately with the desegregation ruling. Many schools remained segregated. In 1957 the federal government sent troops to enforce the *Brown* decision at Little Rock Central High School in Arkansas when black students were admitted for the first time.

After that, nonviolent civil rights protests began throughout the South to allow blacks the right to vote, to sit wherever they chose on buses, to eat at lunch counters, and to attend schools with white students.

In Plains, Georgia, schools were desegregated in 1966 without any violence when two black students enrolled in the high school. It had taken twelve years to honor the court's decision.

*A black student on her way to Little Rock Central High School amid protestors against integration. The National Guard stands in the background.*

*Carter and Rosalynn built a brick home in Plains in*
*which to raise their three sons.*

───────────── ✧ ─────────────

In 1961 the Carter peanut warehouse was doing well.
He and Rosalynn decided they could afford to buy a lot on
Woodland Drive and build a house on it. They were able
to move into their brick home later that year.

## THE POLITICAL LIFE

Carter was asked to run for the U.S. Congress in 1961. He
told the committee of men who came to speak with him
that he had all he could do with his farming and warehouse
operation. He could not leave his responsibilities to go to
Washington, D.C.

But he was getting involved with local politics in spite of
himself. As chairman of the school board, he felt that the
three local white schools in Sumter County should join

together. At the time, each school had separate and limited resources. Together they could provide better services for the five hundred white students who attended them. But the public worried that Carter's idea was an attempt to integrate the schools—to bring in black students—and they voted against it. Meanwhile, the University of Georgia in Athens had admitted two black students in 1962. All around them, the civil rights movement was attempting to bring changes.

In September 1962, the peanut and cotton harvests were larger than usual. When they were not in school, the Carter boys joined their parents at the warehouse along with the other employees. They worked night and day, bringing in tons of peanuts from the local farmers,

*The Carter family (from left to right), Chip, Jack, Rosalynn, Carter, and Jeff, worked as a family to keep the peanut business going.*

checking the seed peanuts that would be used to plant the next year's crop, and ginning the cotton bolls to separate the cotton fiber from the seed. It was the most hectic time of the year, but Carter managed to find time to think while he worked. He decided he wanted to run for the state senate, but he didn't say a word to Rosalynn. He kept the idea to himself.

On October 1, his thirty-eighth birthday, he drove into Americus, Sumter County's seat, to see who was running for the state senate. While he was there, he discovered the county had no candidate. He stopped at the newspaper office and put a notice in the paper that he was a candidate for the Democratic Party's primary election for the Fourteenth Senatorial District. The Fourteenth District in southwestern Georgia was made up of many small rural counties. Americus and Plains were both towns in Sumter County.

Carter knew absolutely nothing about running a political campaign, but he had two weeks to learn before the election. When he told Rosalynn, she was surprised by his decision, but she set to work to help get him elected. She called every name on the county voters' list asking them to vote for Jimmy Carter. She put his sister Gloria to work addressing letters to the voters. She designed posters and business cards. Carter put up the posters and tried to talk to as many people as he could. He spoke on the radio and even on television for the first time.

On the primary's election day, Carter visited many nearby counties to observe the voting. He learned that there were many voting irregularities. For example, in Quitman County, the board of elections had not even set up the voting booths, and the election manager told the voters to scratch out Carter's name and vote for his opponent.

Carter lost the primary, but he was certain the election had not been fair. He decided to contest the results. After hearing Carter's lawyer detail all the illegal actions he had uncovered in the election, a judge threw out the votes—legal and illegal—from the contested precincts. Carter had a slight edge in the votes that remained. He became the Democratic candidate for senator in the November election in the Fourteenth District.

Carter won the November election and had one more hurdle to pass. There was still a chance that his seat would be contested, and the General Assembly (the legislature) in Atlanta would refuse to swear him in. Until the last second, he had no idea about the outcome, but he waited with candidates from the other districts. When his name was called, he was sworn in without a hitch. Then he knew he was a state senator.

Carter had been naive when he began the race. He quickly had learned how much deceit and cheating could be involved in the politics of southwestern Georgia.

## CHAPTER FIVE

# WINNING AND LOSING

*People intimidated by corrupt public officials*
*don't necessarily like it; if given some leadership*
*and a chance, they are willing to stand up and*
*be counted on the side of decency and of honest*
*politics and government.*

—Jimmy Carter

In January 1963, Jimmy Carter moved to the Piedmont Hotel in Atlanta to serve as a state senator. Rosalynn stayed behind in Plains to run the warehouse. He spent the next forty-five days in the state capital as he learned about his new job. When he vowed to read all the bills he would be voting on, he had no idea what an enormous task it would be. To get through the huge number of bills, he taught himself speed-reading techniques. Studying every bill was an important part of being a senator, and he was determined to become the best senator he could be.

After the legislative session was over, Carter moved back to Plains. That summer most Southern cities were divided over civil rights. In Americus a white male student who escorted a black woman to register to vote was attacked by angry men. This was the first of many local protests by blacks and whites. In June 1963, President John Kennedy sent his deputy attorney general Nicholas Katzenbach and other federal authorities to force the admittance of two African American students to the University of Alabama. That night the president spoke to the nation on television: "This is not a sectional issue. . . . Nor is this a partisan issue. . . . We are confronted primarily with a moral issue. It is as old as the scriptures and is as clear as the American Constitution."

Carter and his mother were especially impressed by Kennedy's stand. Miss Lillian had always cared about the African Americans in her community, had nursed their families, and had treated them as her equals. Many others in the South did not share her attitude. When Kennedy was assassinated in November 1963, many people were glad. Carter's son, Chip, was so upset when his teacher told the class she was pleased that Kennedy was dead that he threw his desk at her. Carter found it difficult to discipline Chip since he understood why his son had been so angry.

While Carter served in the Georgia senate, he was able to get more state funding for education. He felt one of his major accomplishments was to see that Georgia Southwestern became a four-year college. With a colleague, he rewrote the Democratic Party rules and on his own searched for ways to save state money and reduce legal delays.

After serving two terms in the state senate, Carter decided he wanted to run for U.S. Congress in 1966. He announced his candidacy in March and began to study methods to remember people's names because he knew this was a way to impress voters. One of his biographers reported that he "developed this skill to a fine art."

## RUNNING FOR GOVERNOR

Carter soon realized that he was most needed in Georgia. On June 12, he announced his decision to run for governor of the state, rather than for the U.S. Congress. Throughout the summer, the whole family worked on the campaign. To

*Rosalynn and the boys spread the word about*
*Carter's candidacy for governor.*

*Carter campaigns for governor at an intersection in Plains.*

work with them, they brought in young, well-educated men with thoughtful new ideas, such as Hamilton Jordan, a student at the University of Georgia, and Bert Lance, a businessman from northern Georgia.

Rosalynn gave birth to their fourth child, Amy Lynn, on October 19, 1967. All three sons were thrilled to have a sister, although they were quite grown-up by the time she was born. Jeff, fifteen, was a junior in high school. Chip was seventeen, and as soon as he graduated from high school, he became an active campaigner for his dad. Jack, at twenty, had just joined the navy.

As hard as they all worked, Carter lost the campaign to Lester Maddox, a well-known segregationist. The *Atlanta Constitution* wrote: "Regardless of Carter's loss, his showing means a new Democratic star is born." But Carter was discouraged about losing the election and about owing money to his friends, who had guaranteed his loans. Worst of all, he had used up most of the family's savings on campaign expenses.

Although Carter knew that he had done his very best in the campaign, his cousin Hugh remembered how he walked "around by himself across his peanut fields, shoulders hunched, looking down at the ground or up at the sky. It was as if he were looking for some answer but there was none."

Carter went back to his study of the Bible and to writings of people he admired. He was searching for answers to the question of how he could stay in politics and remain a moral person. Often he felt that the two were opposing concepts, especially when someone like Maddox could beat him. But once he was feeling better, he knew he had to run for governor again.

## GOVERNOR OF GEORGIA

On Friday, April 3, 1970, at the Georgia state capitol, Jimmy Carter, carrying two-year-old Amy in his arms, made his formal announcement that he was again a candidate for governor. He chose his cousin Hugh to be his campaign chairman and Hamilton Jordan to assist him. Jody Powell, another young Georgia student, volunteered to help because he believed in Carter's political ideas.

Carter studied the 1966 campaign to see why he had lost. It seemed that people didn't know who he was. They kept asking the question, "Jimmy who?" He vowed to make sure that everyone in the state would know who Jimmy Carter was by the time the election came.

Carter worked all day in the peanut warehouse, and then at night, he drove from county to county giving speeches and talking to people. Every time he met someone, he recorded his or her name on a tape recorder. By then it had become a habit for him to keep track of the names of people he met in every community. Rosalynn and his sister Gloria wrote thank-you notes to everyone the next day and kept a file of the names. Carter studied the issues and read every book he could find to stay informed. He wrote his own speeches and tried to keep them personal and specific to each local area he visited. Miss Lillian, who had joined the Peace Corps in 1966 and was sent to India, returned to Plains in time to campaign for her son.

This time Carter felt he had an advantage over his opponent, Carl Sanders, because he was close to the working people of Georgia. Sanders was a country club member who appealed to the wealthy. He had personally benefited financially from his term as governor from 1963 to 1967.

Carter used the peanut as a symbol of his campaign. Men wore gold peanuts in their lapels, and women wore their gold peanuts as pendants. His commercials attempted to show that he was a hardworking farmer who understood what the average person needed.

On Sunday afternoons, all the campaign workers met to share what they had accomplished during the week. Carter gave them pep talks to keep up their spirits. Afterward, they auctioned items that had been donated to the campaign.

They needed every penny. Rosalynn described how they had to borrow cars from supporters for the travels throughout the state. They had to find people to stay with when they went out of town. They made sure to pick up every printed handout to reuse after it was discarded.

She and Carter realized they might have to take out a loan on the farm to finance the campaign. It was a terrible decision to make, because if they lost the election, they lost the farm. But they had no choice.

## GEORGIA'S GOVERNOR

On November 3, Carter won the election, receiving 60 percent of the vote. He was thrilled to be elected, but Lester Maddox had been elected lieutenant governor, and that meant Carter would have to find ways to work with him. Georgia did not allow a person to serve more than one term in a row as governor, so Maddox had devised this way to stay involved in politics. He would become Carter's "biggest headache," as he fought against all of the changes Carter hoped to accomplish for the state of Georgia. Maddox was a bigot. He did not believe in integration and did not respect the rights of all the people of Georgia.

On the wintry afternoon of January 12, 1971, Jimmy Carter was sworn in as the seventy-sixth governor of Georgia. Rain threatened all morning, but when Carter stood up to give his inaugural address, the sun broke through thick clouds. He had written his own speech, as he always did. He began: "It is a long way from Plains to Atlanta." He explained that he had been making the trip for four and one-half years, and he was very glad to have arrived at last.

*Carter* (right, at podium) *takes the oath of office during his inauguration for governor of Georgia on January 12, 1971.*

He continued: "The time for racial discrimination is over. No poor, rural, weak, or black person should ever have to bear the additional burden of being deprived of the opportunity of an education, a job, or simple justice." His whole speech lasted only eight minutes.

Because of his strong stand against racism, Carter's picture was featured on the cover of *Time* magazine on May 31, 1971, to represent the changing face of Southern governors.

Carter was eager to reorganize state government and hoped that he would get strong support for his changes. Lester Maddox fought his attempts and tried to kill the reorganization bill, gathering all the anti-Carter legislators he could find. The newspapers noted the battle lines:

*Lieutenant Governor Lester Maddox (standing)*
*opposed much of Carter's proposed legislation.*

"Carter and Maddox put the political heavyweight championship of Georgia on the line," or "Jimmy and Lester Slug It Out."

Carter spoke on the radio. He sent out pamphlets. He persuaded the legislators of both parties that his bill would be good for the state. The bill reduced government agencies from sixty-five to twenty. It established a simple department of human resources to care for all the medical and social service needs of the people. He was so determined to pass the bill that former secretary of state Ben Fortson said, "Carter reminds me of a South Georgia turtle. He doesn't go around a log. He just sticks his head in the middle and pushes and pushes until the log gives way."

Carter was able to get the bill passed at the last possible minute. He signed it into law on February 15, 1971.

## ACCOMPLISHMENTS

"Jimmy Carter loved being governor," said one of his biographers. He carefully studied every issue. He began a new process of zero-based budgeting for state departments, in which each department head had to start with new budget figures every year. They could not carry over their allotments or hide the figures from the previous year. It was similar to balancing a checkbook and knowing that the figures were correct each month.

Rosalynn, as First Lady of Georgia, worked for mental health causes, and she encouraged her husband to place great emphasis on that area. Carter increased the number of mental health centers in the state from twenty-three to one hundred thirty-four by the time he left office. He also added twenty-three group homes for the mildly retarded.

*Governor Carter and First Lady Rosalynn enjoy a quite moment together.*

Carter cut the administrative costs of the state government in half. Before him, Lester Maddox had given jobs to his friends while he was in office, and there were hundreds of boards and commissions. Carter reduced them to twenty. He took the state money and made sure it was invested in banks and not loaned out to the governor's friends.

Carter prevented a dam from being built on the Flint River, fifty miles southeast of Atlanta. He visited the site several times and learned that the dam would be used only for recreation. It would not benefit the environment, generate electrical power, or control floods as the U.S. Army Corps of Engineers had claimed. Because of this, he gained a reputation for caring about the environment.

Carter established a ten-member commission to select potential judges based on their qualifications so that appointments could not be used to reward political friends. He saved the taxpayers almost $800,000 on telephone bills by having all calls monitored to be sure they were made for government business. He increased the number of African Americans working for the state. When he came into office, only three African Americans served on major state boards and commissions. When he left, there were fifty-three. The number of African American state employees grew from 4,850 to 6,684 during his years as governor.

Carter was not the kind of governor Georgia had had in the past. He didn't socialize with his fellow legislators. He didn't like "horse trading with other legislators, where they gave one thing to gain something else." He believed in working hard and allowing time for his prayers.

One of the ideas he hoped to put into practice came from the writings of the Chinese philosopher, Kuan Tzu,

*Carter* (far right) *appointed many African Americans to Georgia's state boards and commissions.*

who lived about 2000 B.C. It said, "If you give a man a fish, he has one meal. If you teach him how to fish, he can feed himself for life." Jimmy Carter knew that disadvantaged people needed the opportunity to learn skills so they could help themselves.

Carter had a portrait of Martin Luther King Jr. hung in the hall of the Georgia State Capitol as one of his last acts before he left office. He felt it was a "small gesture," but it showed how far the state had come and how much work remained to be done. Outside the building, the Ku Klux Klan paraded against this action. Carter was not "extremely popular when he left office in January, 1975, but he knew that he had done his very best."

## CHAPTER SIX

# HIGHER OFFICE

*Our people are our most precious possession. We
cannot afford to waste the talents and abilities
given by God to one single person.*
—Jimmy Carter

After serving two terms in the Georgia senate and one term as
Georgia's governor, Jimmy Carter felt he had learned how to
make positive changes in people's lives through government.
He decided he was ready to run for president of the United
States. Again, he didn't tell anyone, but he began preparing.
He knew he had to improve his knowledge of foreign affairs,
and he had to have more exposure in states beyond the South.

Carter's first opportunity to become part of the national
scene occurred at the 1972 Democratic National
Convention, when he nominated Senator Henry Jackson
from the state of Washington to be the Democratic presidential candidate. By Christmas of that year, Carter had
told Rosalynn and the family that he was going to run for

president in 1976 and that he would begin to work toward
that election in 1974. They all supported his decision.
Campaigning for Democratic candidates around the country during the midterm elections in 1974 allowed him to
travel from state to state to meet leaders in the party.

## THE CAMPAIGN

Carter made the formal announcement that he was running
for president on December 12, 1974, at the National Press
Club in Washington, D.C. Later that night, he repeated his
intentions in Georgia, at the Atlanta Civic Center. From the
beginning, the family had decided the campaign would require
all of them to work on it. Jack and Chip and their wives went
to New Hampshire, where the first primary would be held.
Jeff, who was at Georgia State University, worked in the

*Three days after his announcement to run for president, Carter
(far right)* appeared on Meet the Press, *a political talk show.*

*Amy stayed in school during the presidential campaign.*

✧ —————————————

Atlanta headquarters. Miss Lillian spoke as often as she could. So did her younger sister, Aunt Sissy, who lived in Maine. Eight-year-old Amy stayed in school in Plains, living with Miss Lillian or Rosalynn's mother when her parents were away campaigning.

Rosalynn started campaigning in Tallahassee, Florida, where no one knew who Jimmy Carter was. It was April 14, 1975, and eighteen months remained until the election. Rosalynn discovered that reporters and radio figures didn't even know what to ask her. So she made a list of questions she thought important and shaped answers that were simple and easily remembered: Jimmy Carter was governor of Georgia. As governor, he balanced the state budget. He has also been a farmer and a businessman. He is an honest man and a Washington outsider who would bring high standards to government.

Carter's brother Billy kept the peanut warehouse going. Cousin Hugh helped whenever he could. When the family campaigned, they all emphasized the same message: Jimmy Carter is an honest man. The public had just lived through the Watergate scandal in Washington, D.C. (Years before

*A campaign button for Carter*

——————— ✧ ———————

aides of Republican president Richard Nixon had broken
the law by hiring people to illegally enter the offices of the
Democratic Party to get information that would help him
win the presidency. Then Nixon and his aides tried to hide
their involvement in the break-in.)

By the time of the Carter campaign, the public had lost
trust in most politicians, but Carter's honesty appealed to
many people. Many were also interested in a politician who
had been able to accomplish so much in his own state. To
capitalize on his honesty and accomplishments, Carter campaigned "on his personality and his character" more than
on the issues.

One of the most important features of his campaign was
the Peanut Brigade formed by Hamilton Jordan, who had
been campaign manager when Carter had run for governor.
The brigade members were Georgians—ninety-eight of

them—who volunteered to travel around the country educating the public about Jimmy Carter. In January 1976, they started out in the extremely cold state of New Hampshire. Knocking on doors of registered voters, they brought the simple message that Jimmy Carter was a good person, a religious man, a good governor who should be the winning candidate. After they reached as many voters as possible, they returned to their own homes in Georgia. They wrote to thank the people they had met, reminding them in their personal note to vote for Carter, just as Carter and Rosalynn had done when he had run for state senate.

The state of Iowa held the first important caucus in January 1976, when Iowans came together on a single evening to select the delegates who would choose the nominees of their party. Carter spent as much time as he could in Iowa and made an effort to meet as many citizens as possible. His efforts proved successful, and he won that caucus by almost 30 percent. In February he moved on to New Hampshire, where his Peanut Brigade had been preparing the way for him. He also won in that state by nearly 30 percent. Separately, Rosalynn and Jimmy Carter moved from state to state. They continued to win delegates from many of the states across the nation: Florida's by 35 percent and Pennsylvania's by 37 percent. But they lost the important Democratic states of California and New Jersey.

By early June, Carter had won primaries and caucuses in enough states to come out ahead of the other Democratic candidates. When he won in Ohio, it gave him a total of 1,260 delegates to the Democratic National Convention, which would be held in New York City. When the other candidates began to drop out, they pledged their delegates to

Carter, and these additional delegates put him over the top with 1,505 votes.

## NOMINATION

On the night of the nomination, Rosalynn sat in the balcony at Madison Square Garden with friends and family, while Carter stayed at the hotel with Miss Lillian and Amy. Candidates traditionally did not appear in the hall until they were nominated. The time-honored counting of delegate votes began. Each state was called in alphabetical order. For example, the Florida delegate rose to inform the convention that this beautiful state, with its beaches and high-rises, its healthy climate, its oranges and grapefruits was casting all its votes for Carter.

Even though Rosalynn thought her husband had enough votes to win the nomination, she said she still had "butterflies in [her] stomach," until the Ohio delegate rose to tell the convention that the Buckeye State, with its technology, culture, and sports contests, rivers and admirable architecture, was casting its 119 votes for Carter! Just as it had in the primaries, the state of Ohio had put Carter over the top to reach 1,505 votes. Rosalynn wished she could be in the hotel room to celebrate that moment with him.

*Carter chose Walter Mondale to run for vice president.*

*Carter and Mondale celebrate after winning the Democratic Party's nomination for president and vice president.*

Early the next morning, Carter called Senator Walter "Fritz" Mondale, the senator from Minnesota, to ask him to be his vice-presidential candidate. An earlier meeting with Mondale had gone smoothly. The two men had agreed on most foreign and domestic issues, and Carter was pleased with how well prepared the senator was for their talk. He knew that Mondale would bring to their partnership needed support from Minnesota, as well as an understanding of Washington politics.

The next night, Carter stood at the podium to speak to the convention. He began, "My name is Jimmy Carter and I'm running for president." These were the very words he had used when he began his campaign. Carter wanted to keep the speech personal, and so he went on to tell the thousands of cheering delegates about his experiences of the

last four years. He repeated his worries that the judicial system did not provide the poor with access to good legal
defense. As pleased as he was by the enthusiasm his speech
received, he knew the real work was just beginning.

When the Democratic Convention ended, the Carters
continued to travel throughout the country to meet the
people and tell their story in the three months remaining
before the election. They hoped to explain Carter's virtues
and why he would make a better president than Gerald
Ford, who was called the "unelected president." (Ford had
become president when President Nixon resigned in 1974,
after the Watergate scandal.) In his campaign, Carter
promised to "restore honesty to the presidency."

Carter invited experts in foreign policy, economics, and
defense to come to Plains to advise him. They all flew into
Atlanta and were driven three hours by chartered bus to
Miss Lillian's Pond House in Plains. Most of them had not

*——————————— ✧*
*Presidential candidate*
*Carter speaks with*
*reporters from the*
*terrace of Miss Lillian's*
*house in Plains.*

ridden in a bus for years, but they were willing to put up with that inconvenience because they wanted to share their ideas with the candidate. Carter asked penetrating questions of the experts and took detailed notes throughout the six-hour sessions.

Then he went outside to talk to the waiting reporters. "Here's what I learned today," he said, giving them in just fifteen minutes precise details about what had been discussed for six hours. The journalists found his ability amazing.

## ELECTION

The election was held on November 2, 1976. The Carters voted early in Plains and then drove to a hotel in Atlanta to wait for results. Family and campaign workers waited nervously with them. The couple held hands as they kept track of the states' electoral votes.

By midnight the election still was not decided. One o'clock. Two o'clock. Three o'clock. At three-thirty in the morning, the governor of Mississippi called to tell Carter that he had carried the state. That win gave him the final seven electoral votes needed to win the election. At the same time, a television announcer proclaimed Carter the projected winner.

Carter thanked his wife and children for all they had done. "It was a long, hard fight and I couldn't have done it without you," he told them. "I'm proud of all of you." Carter and his wife both shed tears when they arrived home in Plains later that morning and faced their welcoming friends.

# ELECTORAL COLLEGE

The president of the United States is not elected by popular vote. Each state is assigned electors in the Electoral College based on the total number of representatives and senators of that state. A state with a large population, such as New York, with more members in the House of Representatives, has more electoral votes than Wyoming, with a small population and one representative. The electors meet after the general election to cast their votes. They usually vote for the candidate who won the election in the state they represent. The Electoral College officially decides who will be the next president.

In 1976 when Jimmy Carter ran for president against Gerald Ford, Carter won the election by a narrow margin. Only 54 percent of the population came out to vote that year. Of that number, Carter won almost 50 percent of the popular vote and 297 electoral votes. Ford came close with nearly 48 percent of the popular vote and 240 electoral votes.

In some elections, such as the one in 2000, the winner of the popular vote didn't win the election. Al Gore received the highest number of popular votes in 2000, but George W. Bush won the election by winning in the states with more electoral votes.

*Jimmy Carter takes the oath of office as president of the United States.*

## CHAPTER SEVEN

# THE WHITE HOUSE

*When my time as your President has
ended . . . I would hope that the nations of the
world might say that we had built a lasting
peace, based not on weapons of war but on
international policies which reflect our own
most precious values.*

—Jimmy Carter

On Inauguration Day, January 20, 1977, Jimmy and
Rosalynn Carter woke early in Blair House, the presidential
guest house, where they were staying until they could move
into the White House. It was freezing cold outside, and
they heard the soldiers using jackhammers to break up ice
that had formed overnight on the sidewalks.

The whole family attended a service at the First Baptist
Church before taking a limousine to the Capitol Building.
As they approached the flag-draped platform where the
inauguration would be held, a U.S. Marine band played the

"Navy Hymn" in honor of Carter's years in the navy. Flags snapped in the wind. The crowds applauded as the Carters found their seats. Amy moved over to sit on Rosalynn's lap, perhaps overwhelmed by the huge number of people around them.

Soon Rosalynn moved Amy to her own seat and rose to hold the Bible Miss Lillian had given her son. Jimmy Carter, swearing on that Bible, took the oath of office to become the thirty-ninth president of the United States.

In his brief eight-minute speech, Carter promised to make a "commitment to human rights," and to bring about "the elimination of all nuclear weapons from this earth." He quoted from the prophet Micah in the Old Testament Bible: "He hath showed thee, O man, what is good; and what doth the Lord require of thee, but to do justly and to love mercy, and to walk humbly with thy God."

Then instead of getting back into their waiting limousine, he and Rosalynn, again holding hands, began walking along Pennsylvania Avenue. They were on their way to the White House, literally taking the biblical passage to heart.

"They're walking! They're walking!" many in the surprised crowds shouted. Nine-year-old Amy skipped along, sometimes with them and sometimes with her brothers who were walking behind. The people waiting along the way held signs and cheered as they saw their new president and his family leading the parade on foot. "It was one of those few perfect moments in life when everything seems absolutely right," Carter later said.

As soon as Carter arrived at the White House, he was eager to see the Oval Office, where he would be working, but he didn't know where it was. He told a Secret

*The Carters walk down Pennsylvania Avenue to the White House after the presidential inauguration.*

Service agent where he was going. Then he followed the agent outside, down the covered walkway, and into a large room. Left there alone, Carter scrutinized every detail of the Oval Office, almost afraid to touch anything. Finally, he gathered courage and opened the drapes to let in the sunlight.

## GETTING DOWN TO WORK

Carter's first act as president was to sign an executive order granting amnesty to draft evaders. These were men who had refused, for moral reasons, to serve in the Vietnam War. They hid or fled the country when they were called to duty. On his first day in the Oval Office, Carter met with Vietnam veteran Max Cleland, who had been injured in the war and was in a wheelchair. Cleland warned Carter that senate members were against his amnesty plan. Leaning down, Carter told Cleland, "I don't care if all 100 of them are against me. It's the right thing to do."

There was a huge public outcry against his amnesty order in the beginning, but Carter was determined that it was crucial to healing the nation, which had been divided by the country's participation in the war. Soon after, the order was seen as a sign of strength. Carter had followed his deepest convictions, despite the controversy the amnesty created.

Carter also wanted to be closer to the people, so in his first months in office he eliminated many of the displays of power previous presidents had used. He chose to carry his own suit bag when he traveled, he did not allow the playing of "Hail to the Chief" when he appeared, and he requested

*During Carter's no-frills presidency, he carried his own luggage when traveling on presidential business.*

that the presidential yacht be sold. He and Rosalynn also decided that Amy should go to a public school in Washington, D.C. Carter hoped to maintain this "simpler lifestyle" with a policy he called "No ruffles and flourishes."

## PARTNERS IN THE WHITE HOUSE

As first lady, Rosalynn Carter planned to continue working to support mental health legislation. To learn what was needed, she traveled around the country listening to people's concerns. Later, Carter established a Presidential Commission on Mental Health and Mental Retardation to make recommendations for improved care.

Rosalynn also sat in on meetings of Carter's cabinet (the people who headed various federal departments). She took notes but never spoke. Her presence was shocking to many, but she justified it by saying that listening to the discussions enabled her to be an active adviser to her husband. Because both Carters felt it was important, they ignored the controversy it created.

## WOMEN IN GOVERNMENT

As he had promised in his campaign, Carter selected many women to serve in the government. He appointed three women to serve in his cabinet when only three women had been appointed to these positions in all previous administrations combined. He appointed forty-one women to serve as federal judges, when only five women had been appointed in the past. He also appointed sixteen women as ambassadors, when only nine had been appointed before. He found that increasing the number of women in government was an easy promise to keep.

*Carter named three women to serve in his Cabinet.*

---

### FOREIGN RELATIONS

One of Carter's dreams as president was to eliminate all nuclear weapons. He and Soviet leader Leonid Brezhnev signed the SALT II Treaty, which had been in negotiation for almost six years under two previous U.S. presidents. Under the treaty, both nations agreed to begin reducing stockpiles of nuclear weapons.

Carter also pledged to turn over control of the Panama Canal to Panama by the end of 1999, because it was the right thing to do. (In 1903 the United States had taken a ten-mile strip of land in Panama on which to build the Panama Canal and continued to control it, without ever receiving the formal consent of the Panamanian government.) Many Americans wanted to maintain control of the canal to protect it from being used by future enemies of the United States. Carter's canal treaty passed the senate by a single vote.

As a young submariner, Carter had visited China. He liked the people there, just as his uncle Tom Gordy had when he had sent postcards from China to young Jimmy. While he was president, Carter worked to have the United States open diplomatic relations with the Communist government in China and to foster trade between the two countries. He built on the friendly exchanges Richard Nixon had established with China during his presidency and developed a warm relationship with China's leader, Deng Xiaoping.

*Carter meets with China's leader Deng Xiaoping.*

## CHAPTER EIGHT

# CAMP DAVID ACCORDS

*Some of the most unpleasant experiences*
*of my life occurred during these days—*
*and, of course, one of the most gratifying*
*achievements came at the end of it.*
—Jimmy Carter

Another one of Jimmy Carter's dreams as president was to bring about peace in the Middle East. Ever since Israel had been declared a state by the United Nations in 1948, Israel and the neighboring Arab countries had been at war. The Arab nations refused to recognize the existence of Israel or to negotiate with its leaders.

In November 1977, Anwar al-Sadat, president of the mainly Arab country of Egypt, took the courageous step of going to Jerusalem to meet with Israeli prime minister Menachem Begin. While there, Sadat spoke before the Knesset, the governing body of Israel, saying, "Tell your sons that the past war was the last of wars and the end of sorrows."

Shortly after his visit, Sadat invited Begin to visit him in Egypt for further talks. President Jimmy Carter saw these meetings as a breakthrough for ending thirty years of war between the two countries and perhaps for changing the way the other Arab states dealt with Israel.

## AT CAMP DAVID

In July of 1978, as the Carters were walking through the woods at Camp David, the presidential retreat in Maryland, Carter turned to Rosalynn and said, "It's so beautiful here. I believe if I could get Sadat and Begin both here together, we could work out some of the problems between them." He invited President Anwar al-Sadat and Prime Minister Menachem Begin to meet with him at Camp David. Both men promptly agreed to come.

President Sadat and his delegation arrived by helicopter on Tuesday, September 5, about three o'clock in the afternoon. Prime Minister Begin arrived two hours later. Carter met with Begin that night and assured him that he was committed to Israel's security.

The following morning Carter met with President Sadat, who said his first priority was that the Sinai Peninsula, land captured from Egypt by the Israelis, should be returned to Egypt. Next, he wanted Israeli settlements removed from this area.

Carter and his team worked all day on Saturday preparing a U.S. plan that would take Israeli and Egyptian needs into account. "Now all we have to do is get both sides to agree to sign it!" the president said. He thought the summit would last only three or four days. It was already day five!

*Carter (center), Menachem Begin (right), and Anwar al-Sadat (left) meet at Camp David to discuss prospects of peace between Egypt and Israel.*

———————————— ✧ ————————————

On Sunday, Carter suggested that they take a trip to nearby Gettysburg, Pennsylvania, one of the most famous the Civil War battlefields. As they neared the historical battlefield, Begin and Sadat said that they both had been jailed as political prisoners and that one of the most difficult aspects of their imprisonment had been being deprived of books. Sadat said he meditated in his cell all day and night. Begin said for him "the prison was a university." He taught history and languages to his cellmates.

They were both familiar with the Civil War history of the United States. They knew about the battle that had taken place at Gettysburg. As they approached the battlefield, Begin began reciting Abraham Lincoln's Gettysburg Address.

Sadat found it meaningful that the United States had been able to heal the wounds between North and South after the Civil War. He hoped that Israel and Egypt would be able to "move confidently toward an era of peace."

For three days, Carter moved between discussions with the Egyptian and Israeli delegations, without reaching an agreement. The differences were narrowing, but major issues still remained to resolve.

By September 14—day ten—the whole process seemed in danger of abruptly ending. And September 15—day eleven—Carter learned that Sadat was packing his clothes to return to Egypt. Carter prayed for guidance, then rushed to Sadat's cabin where he pleaded with the Egyptian leader to stay as proof of their close personal friendship. Carter promised that if Israel or Egypt later rejected any agreement that was made, he would tear up the proposals Sadat had agreed to. Sadat answered, "If you give me this statement, I will stick with you to the end."

On September 16—day twelve—Carter walked with Sadat early in the morning and came back to his desk to work out more details. He wrote out a new draft and showed it to Sadat that afternoon. After their meeting, he made additional changes and wrote another clean draft.

That afternoon Prime Minister Begin visited Carter in his study. Dinnertime came and went. Rosalynn waited for them to come out. More time passed. She sent them cheese and crackers to eat. Still, they didn't come out. Finally, at midnight, Begin left the study to return to his own cabin. The president felt they had made great progress.

## AGREEMENT AT LAST

In the morning, Carter told the delegations that this day, Sunday, September 17, 1978, would be the last day of the summit whether they came to an agreement or not. He told them that he had put aside all the responsibilities he had as president for the past twelve days and that he had to go back to Washington to resume the work of the country.

They still had to discuss the future of Jerusalem and the Israeli settlements. At the last moment, Begin said that he would ask the Knesset to agree to withdraw the settlers from the Sinai Peninsula and to prohibit new settlements there. He also agreed that the goal was to have an undivided Jerusalem that would be a "city of peace, holy to Judaism, Christianity, and Islam . . . [and] that all persons would have free access to it."

There were no further obstacles. Begin and Sadat said they would sign a joint agreement. After the terms of the agreement were put in place, Israel and Egypt would have normal relations with each other, allowing their citizens to trade and to travel between the two countries. Thirty years of war between them would be ended.

The Carters and all of the foreign officials rushed to their cabins to pack and take helicopters back to Washington. At ten o'clock that Sunday evening, the three leaders met in the East Room of the White House to sign the agreement they had been working on for thirteen days. All three of them realized what a historic moment it was.

According to Moshe Dayan, an Israeli delegate to the conference, "There had never been a President in the past willing to devote as much time to an all-out effort as President Carter." Dayan said that he had been part of every negotiation involving Israel since the state was established. But never before had there been negotiations for peace. Always there were negotiations regarding borders and

*Carter oversees the signing of the groundbreaking peace treaty between Israel and Egypt.*

land rights. Perhaps, there really would be peace. That was everyone's hope.

In March of the following year, the two leaders returned to Washington to sign a peace treaty between Israel and Egypt. Both Begin and Sadat had made enormous sacrifices by coming to Camp David for the summit. Begin was harshly criticized by his own party when he returned to Israel, and many there felt he had threatened Israel's security. Sadat "had taken real risks" when he visited Jerusalem and "turned the entire Arab world against him." (When Sadat was assassinated just three years later, Carter knew his death was the result of his having signed a peace treaty with Israel. Although peace throughout the region has been elusive, Israel and Egypt have since maintained a peaceful relationship.)

# ARAB-ISRAELI CONFLICT

In A.D. 70, the Romans conquered ancient Israel and destroyed the temple in the capital city of Jerusalem. Jewish people were dispersed throughout the Roman Empire. For the next two thousand years, they dreamed of returning to Jerusalem.

In the 1890s, Jews began emigrating to Palestine (the name of ancient Israel in modern times) to escape persecution in Europe. On the whole, they lived in peace with their Arab neighbors. Great Britain gained control of the area in 1918 at the end of World War I (1914–1918).

After World War II (1939–1945), Jewish survivors of the Holocaust, Hitler's plan to destroy all Jews, were eager to leave Europe and settle in Palestine. The British government was reluctant to allow hundreds of thousands of Jewish survivors to emigrate. It believed that such large numbers of new settlers would cause conflict with the Arabs who already lived there.

In 1947 the United Nations General Assembly called for the creation of two separate states in Palestine, one Arab and one Jewish. On May 14, 1948, the Jews who had already settled in the area proclaimed it the State of Israel. Arab neighbors were violently against the partition of Palestine. Egypt, Jordan, Syria, Lebanon, and Iraq invaded the new State of Israel. Israel fought back, and to protect its borders, it took control of some of the territory that had been set aside for the Palestinians. Refugees, both Arab and Jewish, resulted from that war. Israel absorbed the Jewish refugees. The Palestinians were kept in refugee camps, and Jordan was the only country to grant them citizenship.

In 1949 an armistice went into effect signed by all of the countries involved except Iraq. That same year, Israel became the fifty-ninth member of the United Nations.

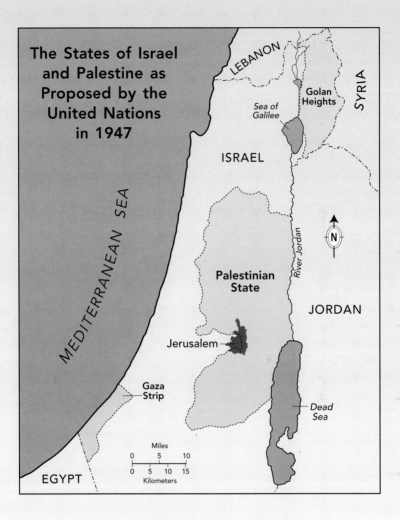

The States of Israel and Palestine as Proposed by the United Nations in 1947

On June 5, 1967, Israel launched a defensive strike against the Egyptian army, which was massing on its border. In what was called the Six-Day War, Israel captured Palestinian land in the Gaza Strip, the West Bank (of the Jordan River), and East Jerusalem. In 1968 Egypt continued its attacks along the banks of the Suez Canal. The two countries finally accepted a cease-fire in 1970.

In 1973 Egypt and Syria attacked Israel again on Yom Kippur, the holiest day of the Jewish year. During the Yom Kippur War, Israel pushed back their advances. Then in 1977, Egyptian president Anwar al-Sadat traveled to Israel, and Israeli prime minister Menachem Begin visited Egypt. In 1978 Jimmy Carter invited Sadat and Begin to Camp David. The Camp David Accords were signed officially on March 26, 1979. Egypt recognized the State of Israel, and Israel resolved to return to Egypt the part of the Sinai Peninsula it had occupied in 1967.

A Palestinian uprising began in 1987 on the West Bank and in the Gaza Strip. Palestinians demonstrated against Israel's military rule in the Palestinian territories and refused to pay taxes to Israel. Most of the protests were peaceful, but some demonstrations turned violent.

In 1993 Palestinian and Israeli leaders started a series of secret peace talks. They came to an agreement in September in Washington, D.C. Palestinian leaders affirmed their recognition of Israel, and Israel promised to move Jewish settlements from parts of the West Bank and the Gaza Strip.

U.S. president Bill Clinton presided over more peace talks in July of 2000. This time, Israeli and Palestinian leaders could not reach an agreement. Control over the city of Jerusalem was the stumbling block. Both Palestinian leader Yasser Arafat and Israeli leader Ehud Barak refused give up rule of certain parts of the city, holy to both Jews and Arabs. Cross-border fighting has continued in the West Bank and Gaza Strip since the talks. Both groups remain hopeful for peace, but violence in the region continues to discourage attempts at successful diplomacy.

## HOSTAGE CRISIS

For many years, the United States had maintained a friendly relationship with Iran, because Iran was a source of much-needed oil. In November of 1977, Carter had invited the Shah of Iran, Mohammad Reza Pahlavi, to the White House.

At that meeting, Carter criticized the Iranian leader for treating his people so harshly. He hoped he could help bring about political and social change in Iran while he maintained a relationship with the shah. Carter had always

*Mohammad Reza Pahlavi*
——————— ✧ ———————

believed that something positive could come from talking to other leaders, even if they were considered dictators or enemies of the United States.

By the following year, the Iranian people could no longer stand the government's repression. When the shah declared martial law, using the military to restrict people's freedoms, they rose up against him and forced him to leave his country. An elderly Muslim religious leader, the Ayatollah Ruhollah Khomeini, had been forced into exile in France by the shah. He returned to Iran to take over leadership of the government.

In November 1979, thousands of Iranian students, followers of Khomeini, invaded the U.S. embassy in Tehran

*Ayatollah Ruhollah Khomeini*
——— ◇ ———

and captured sixty-six Americans who worked there. The students were angry that the United States had aided the shah. They were also angry that Carter had allowed the shah to enter the United States for cancer treatment that October. Carter immediately asked banks to hold onto Iranian assets in the United States, so that these investments could not be used by the hostage takers.

Carter refused to bargain with the militant students. The students wanted to trade the hostages for weapons. They demanded that the shah's assets in the United States be paid to their leader, Khomeini. And they insisted that the United States not interfere in Iranian affairs. Fourteen hostages were released, but fifty-two still remained locked in the U.S. embassy.

Carter decided he could not continue campaigning for a second term as president. "While the crisis continues I must be present to define and lead our response to an ever-changing situation of the greatest security, sensitivity, and importance."

Not only did Carter decide he couldn't leave the White House to campaign, he did not feel comfortable going home to Plains for Christmas. The Carters would have to

*On November 9, 1979, demonstrators in Iran protest the U.S. involvement in Iranian affairs by burning the American flag.*

─────────── ✧ ───────────

break their twenty-six-year tradition of spending Christmas in Plains. Instead, he and Rosalynn decided to spend a few days at Camp David. They invited the White House staff to join them for Christmas dinner.

Before they left for Camp David, the annual Christmas tree-lighting ceremony was held on the south lawn of the White House. It was freezing cold, but still the crowd gathered around the Carters, expecting to see the enormous tree fill the night with its many glowing lights. This was an annual custom, and nothing would keep people away. Carter gave his daughter, Amy, a signal. She pulled the switch. "The crowds gasped," Rosalynn later said. Only a single star—the Star of Hope—at the top of the tree was lit. Nearby, there were rows of small trees, one for each hostage, decorated with soft, blue lights. "We will turn on the other lights when our hostages come home, safe and free," Carter explained.

Some of his advisers wanted him to take military action against Iran, and he was "tempted to lash out," as he called it. But he felt that action would inevitably lead to getting all of the hostages killed.

## PROBLEMS IN AFGHANISTAN

In addition to the crisis with Iran, the Soviet Union sent eighty-five thousand troops into Afghanistan two days after Christmas. Afghanistan adjoins Pakistan and Iran. Carter described the people of Afghanistan as "freedom-loving." He felt that the Soviets wanted to expand their influence over that country because it was near an area rich in oil. The invasion forced Carter to take major steps to show the Soviets how wrong their action was. First, he tabled the Salt II Treaty, which he had negotiated with the Soviet leader, Leonid Brezhnev. This was the agreement to begin reducing stockpiles of weapons in each country. He had already signed Salt II and had expected the Senate to vote for it. Instead, he would ask the Senate not to consider it at all.

Another way he chose to show his anger with the Soviets was to ask the Olympic Committee not to hold the scheduled 1980 Olympic Games in Moscow. When the committee wouldn't agree to move to another site, Carter refused to allow U.S. athletes to participate in the event.

These events were consuming Carter's energy and time. Even without campaigning, though, he won the Iowa

Democratic caucus and then the New Hampshire, Florida, and Illinois primaries. But every night, the news programs reminded him and the American people of his failure in Iran by announcing the number of days the hostages had been in captivity.

By April, when the hostages had been held more than 150 days, Carter agreed to a rescue attempt. He and his advisers thought they could send in special troops by helicopters and planes, rescue the hostages, and escape without any loss of life. But the action was a terrible failure. Eight men were killed when a U.S. airplane and a helicopter collided. This crash derailed any attempt to try to reach the hostages.

——————————————— ✧ ———————————————

*A helicopter and an airplane lie in ruins after the failed rescue attempt of the U.S. hostages in Iran.*

*Republican candidate Ronald Reagan wears a cowboy hat while speaking to a crowd in New Holland, Pennsylvania.*
✧ ——————————————

## A NEW ELECTION

After winning renomination as the Democratic candidate, Carter faced a tough campaign against the Republican nominee, Ronald Reagan. The country liked Reagan's positive attitude, his warmth, and his smiling manner, despite the fact that he glossed over specific ideas about governing the country. For the past four years, Carter had been telling the people that they had to make sacrifices, such as giving up the Panama Canal and conserving oil by using less energy for heat and light. As a symbol of this conservation effort, Carter kept the White House cool and wore a sweater to keep warm when he spoke to the public.

Carter lost the 1980 election to Ronald Reagan. Reagan won 489 Electoral College votes to Carter's 49 electoral votes. Former secretary of state Henry Kissinger said that the American people didn't want a president who wore a sweater. He thought they wanted a "more majestic" figure to govern them.

## POST ELECTION

In his last months as president, Carter had important work to do. He still hoped to arrange for the hostages to return home.

It meant unfreezing assets belonging to Iran and arranging new loans so that the Iranian leaders would be willing to negotiate the hostages' safety. He encouraged Congress to pass a bill that would provide money to clean up chemical dump sites throughout the United States. He signed the Alaska Land Bill, which almost tripled the amount of land in that state that was designated as wilderness.

In his farewell speech to the nation, Carter stressed what he felt had been his major concerns while he had been president: the protection of the environment, nuclear disarmament, and human rights. He did not discuss his disappointment over losing the election but said he hoped that the new administration would also consider these issues as crucial to the future of the United States.

Carter had hoped to see the hostages released while he was still president, but that did not happen. Iranian leaders kept changing their requirements for how they wanted their assets returned, and day after day passed without any agreement. It was not until Ronald Reagan took the oath of office that Carter received notice the hostages were free and on an airplane headed to Wiesbaden, West Germany. After a few days of rest and physical examinations, they would be coming home—all fifty-two of them, safe and sound after 443 days of captivity.

The Carters left Washington for Plains late on the day of Reagan's inauguration. Early the next morning, a helicopter landed on the softball field in Plains. It would take Carter to the airplane bound for Wiesbaden, where he would meet the hostages at last. He admitted that the hostages "sometimes seemed like part of my own family. . . . More than anything else, I wanted those American prisoners to be free."

## CHAPTER NINE

# PRIVATE CITIZEN

*I will lay down my official responsibilities in
this office to take up once more the only title
in our democracy superior to that of President:
the title of citizen.*

—Jimmy Carter

The people of Plains, Georgia, welcomed Jimmy and
Rosalynn Carter home. About three thousand of them lined
up on Main Street's one long block, many of them close
friends and supporters. Even the pouring rain did not keep
them away. They had prepared "the world's largest covered-
dish dinner," and they were going to share it with their
returning neighbors.

"I never doubted that this is where I belong," Carter
told the crowd. He greeted everyone from a platform in
front of the old train depot, where he earlier had
announced his plans to run for president. He shared the
good news that the hostages had been released but said that

he still felt great sadness about the eight lives lost during the rescue attempt. After they tasted many of the casseroles, he and Rosalynn danced to the music of the "Tennessee Waltz" and then walked a few blocks to their home on Woodland Drive.

Carter had discovered that the peanut warehouse he had built "through sheer grit" was now one million dollars in debt and would have to be sold. But he was determined to find a way to keep the family's two thousand acres of land. It held the Carter cemetery with family headstones from the 1800s, as well as graves of former slaves.

## MEMOIRS

Carter knew that he and Rosalynn had to earn money, and friends recommended they both write memoirs of their White House years. Carter planned to spend the next year doing just that.

He had already written *Why Not the Best?* during the presidential campaign, and by the time he left the White House, the book had sold almost one million copies. Carter said he wrote it in "peanut farmer language," using any spare moment he found to write while traveling around the country. He kept detailed diaries amounting to five thousand typewritten pages while he was in the White House, and he drew on those pages for his memoir. But he didn't like to sit at his desk all day long. He liked to steal away to his new workshop with the woodworking equipment his cabinet and staff had given him when he left the White House. In his earlier years, Carter had never found enough time to craft furniture, as he loved to do.

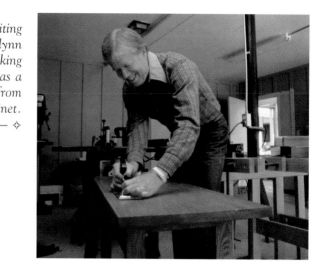

*Carter built a writing table for Rosalynn using the woodworking tools given to him as a farewell gift from members of his cabinet.*

———————— ✧

He also found time for fly-fishing with Rosalynn in Turniptown Creek near the log cabin they were building in northwestern Georgia. For both of them "fly fishing was a spiritual endeavor." They could get out into the running water of the creek, surrounded by trees, away from responsibility, and cast their lines.

Carter completed his book, *Keeping Faith: Memoirs of a President* in 1981. He tried to keep it a personal rather than an analytical look at his presidency. Later, as he traveled to major cities around the country on a book tour, everyone wanted to know if he was enjoying his new life, and Carter answered truthfully, "I'd still rather be president."

Rosalynn's book, *First Lady from Plains,* was on the best-seller list for eighteen weeks and received extremely positive reviews. One writer said that Rosalynn Carter "had developed endurance and toughness to match her husband's." She became a Distinguished Fellow of the Emory

University Institute for Women's Studies in Atlanta. Jimmy Carter was appointed a Distinguished Professor at Emory in 1982.

## WORLD TRAVELERS WITH A WORLD VIEW

As they had promised, both Anwar al-Sadat and Menachem Begin came to visit the Carters in Plains. The Carters also began to travel. On their first foreign trip, they flew to China, where Carter had earlier opened normal diplomatic relations between the United States and China. A state dinner was held to honor Carter and to show him how the Chinese people revered him.

Next, he and Rosalynn traveled to Japan. There Carter "was seen as a peacemaker, not as a failed American ex-president." The Japanese thought of him as a "humble wise man of deep honesty and integrity, unusual in the world of politics."

When Anwar al-Sadat was assassinated in October 1981, Carter felt as though he had lost a brother. He went to the funeral in Egypt with other government officials, including former president Gerald Ford. He and Ford began a friendship that would grow over the years.

The Carters then got involved in Habitat for Humanity. This organization had been founded in 1976 by Millard Fuller, a successful businessman who wanted to use his money to provide shelter for "impoverished people throughout the world." In the spring of 1982, he asked the Carters to help build homes in Americus, Georgia. Then they spent a week in New York City with members of the Plains Maranatha Baptist Church and other volunteers from around the state. They all slept on bunks in a New York

*Putting his carpentry skills to the test through Habitat for Humanity, Carter works on a house in Atlanta. Rosalynn pitches in.*

City church and worked to renovate a dilapidated building on the Lower East Side of New York.

Eventually, Carter led a yearly Habitat for Humanity project in different locations around the country, building homes for poor families in the United States. He has traveled to cities in Latin America and Africa as well.

At about this time, Carter's intrepid mother, Miss Lillian, died at the age of eighty-five. Much of Jimmy Carter's moral toughness was inspired by his mother's life of service and caring for all.

## CARTER CENTER

While working on his memoirs, Carter also was planning for the future. In addition to building a presidential library, Carter wanted to create a setting where government leaders could meet together to talk about their differences and to resolve conflicts. He chose land outside Atlanta for a center that could become a place for "waging peace."

The Carter Center opened its permanent facilities in 1986 on Carter's birthday, October 1, after operating for four years on the Emory University campus. Carter wrote that the "Center's mission is to advance peace and health in neighborhoods and nations around the world. . . . We work alongside the world's forgotten people—those who are the most in need and underserved." He stressed that human rights would be the underlying theme for any work the center carried out.

When requested, the center has provided monitors for elections in countries such as Venezuela in South America, Nigeria in Africa, and Indonesia in Asia, as well as in the United States when the Cherokee Nation held Tribal Council elections in Oklahoma. The goals were always to assure that the elections would be peaceful and the results would be accurate.

—————————————— ✧ ——————————————

*Jimmy and Rosalynn Carter welcome reporters at a reception prior to the opening of the Carter Center.*

Carter also began a campaign against tobacco use, especially because his father and all his siblings had died of pancreatic cancer. They had been heavy smokers, and he had learned that smokers had twice the risk of developing pancreatic cancer than nonsmokers. He insisted there would be no smoking in the Carter Center.

## GLOBAL WORK

Physician Peter Bourne, who worked for the United Nations, made Carter aware of the dangers of the guinea worm. This worm was found in contaminated water in many poor countries throughout the world. The larva live in the body for a year. Then it emerges from a victim's feet as an enormously long worm. As it emerges, it causes blisters on the skin of the feet that are horribly crippling. Carter decided the Carter Center should attempt to educate the leaders of those countries with guinea worm outbreaks on how to clean contaminated water.

By December of 1995, ten years after he began his work on the problem, guinea worm had been almost totally eliminated. When the Carters traveled to Nigeria in 1995, excited children had made signs to welcome them. One sign said, "Guinea worm you better go away. President Carter is coming!"

Carter's next venture was to found Global 2000 with an agricultural expert from the United States and a wealthy Japanese industrialist. (The organization eventually became part of the Carter Center.) This program's aim was to improve conditions for developing countries. It was obvious that poor people could not be interested in democratic elections if they could not feed their families.

In Ghana the Global 2000 team was able to show farmers how to improve their crops. Within five years, the country was feeding its own population, and its president, Jerry Rawlings, allowed democratic elections to take place.

## SEARCHING FOR PEACE

Problems in the Middle East continued to be important to Jimmy Carter. He traveled there in late 1992 and met with Yasser Arafat, head of the Palestine Liberation Organization, which represented Arab people living in Palestine. Arafat reported on a meeting in Oslo, Norway, where he and Israel's prime minister Yitzhak Rabin had agreed upon a Declaration of Principles. Arafat had agreed to renounce terrorism, and the Israelis had agreed to grant the Palestinians a homeland.

In September 1993, Arafat and Rabin went to Washington to sign the declaration on the same table used for the earlier Camp David agreement. As Carter watched the signing, he was deeply moved and didn't bother to wipe away a tear. "The whole world saw the tear," said Dr. Abdul-Karim Iryandi, foreign minister of Yemen. The world also saw the handshake between Arafat and Rabin, two men who had long been enemies.

One of the most important elections Carter monitored for the Carter Center was the first PLO election for a Palestinian Parliament Council. It was held in Jerusalem in January 1996. Most of the cities had an 80 percent voter turnout. Throughout election day, Carter and the other monitors traveled from poll to poll, observing the voting. He had seen irregularities in his own early elections in Georgia, and he was on the lookout for any of the same problems.

*Carter greets newly elected Palestinian president Yasser Arafat
after overseeing Palestinian elections in 1996.*

As expected, Yasser Arafat won the election. He received
88 percent of the vote, and his party won 75 percent of the
council seats. It seemed that the Palestinians had an elected
leader and would soon have an official state separate from
Israel. But that happy moment did not last long. Within
months, Arab terrorists, who still had not accepted the
nation of Israel, began killing Israeli citizens, and peaceful
days were over.

### TRIP TO CUBA

During his presidency, Jimmy Carter had tried to improve
relations with the Caribbean island nation of Cuba. In a
speech to students at Emory University,  he said, "The
most sensitive political issue in our country is Cuba." He
was aware that little progress had occurred in normalizing
relations with that country. In 1959 Fidel Castro had over-
thrown the Cuban dictator, Fulgensio Batista, and had set

up a Communist government. The United States broke off
diplomatic relations with Cuba soon after.

Fidel Castro invited Carter to visit Cuba, and in May
2002, Carter made the trip. No U.S. president had visited
Cuba since Fidel Castro had become dictator. Carter said
his goal was to tell the Cuban people that they were entitled to a democratic existence.

President Castro, wearing a business suit rather than his
usual green military uniform, met Carter and his party at
the airport. Castro assured the Carter group that they
would be allowed to speak to anyone they wished and to go
wherever they chose. This was unusual in Cuba, a totalitar-
ian country where people have few freedoms.

In an ornate hall at the University of Havana,
Carter gave a speech he wrote and delivered entirely
in Spanish. It was carried by television to the whole

Cuban population.
This was an amaz-
ing moment—a for-
mer U.S. president
allowed to speak to
a Communist coun-
try. In his speech,

———————————✧

*Carter and Cuban
president Fidel Castro
shake hands after Carter's
arrival in Cuba.*

Carter praised Castro for the fine health care and education available to the Cuban people. But he boldly pointed out that the people lacked freedom to disagree with the government and to elect their leaders. "I want the people of the United States and Cuba to share more than a love of baseball and wonderful music," Carter told them. He also said he hoped that the U.S. ban on trade with Cuba would be lifted and that the two countries would be able to travel and trade freely with each other. Alfredo Duran, a Cuban American, spoke for many Cubans when he said that Carter had given people hope just by going to Cuba.

## RECOGNITION

Jimmy Carter has grown to be more popular with each passing year. He was honored when he learned that his present home in Plains and his boyhood home in Archery were designated national historic sites, along with the Plains railroad depot, where he began and ended his political life. His old Plains High School became a visitors' center for the many tourists who continue to arrive in town. He and Rosalynn still supervise the crops growing on their lands, but they don't expect their children or grandchildren to be as passionate about farming as they are.

Carter has written that he and Rosalynn have been "full partners in every major decision" since they were first married. That has not changed since they left the White House. Never needing material wealth, they manage to live well on the proceeds from their books and his presidential pension. Their one luxury is taking the whole family—their children and eleven grandchildren—on an outing after Christmas every year.

Jimmy Carter is a religious man. But he doesn't just talk about his faith. He lives it in such visible roles as monitoring elections, preventing disease, and working for Habitat for Humanity. He also lives it in less visible roles, such as teaching classes at Maranatha Baptist Church and mowing its lawn, serving on church committees, and carving wooden collection plates that are passed during services.

His work all over the world has often been recognized, especially with the Nobel Peace Prize in 2002. His books are popular and usually reach the best-seller lists. He is asked to speak throughout the world.

Carter has written books about his early life and his presidency. He is also the author of a book of poems, a book for young people describing his conflict-solving methods, and even a children's picture book, *The Little Baby Snoogle-Fleejer,* illustrated by his daughter, Amy. He has also published a novel about the Revolutionary War as it took place in and around Georgia, entitled *The Hornet's Nest.*

Tip O'Neill, one of his political colleagues, called him the "smartest public official I've ever known." Katharine Graham, a Washington publisher, agreed. She stated, "Carter is by far the most intelligent president in my lifetime."

Perhaps, he was not able to accomplish all he hoped to while he was president—circumstances were against him. But he has used his great intelligence and compassion for the good of the world, and as he grows older, he has gained greater respect and is more revered than ever.

No wonder a young boy in a *New Yorker* cartoon tells his father he wants to be an ex-president when he grows up! Jimmy Carter has made the role admirable. He is a superb ex-president.

# TIMELINE

**1924**  James "Jimmy" Carter II is born in Plains, Georgia.

**1927**  Eleanor Rosalynn Smith is born.

**1946**  Carter graduates from Annapolis. Carter and Rosalynn are married.

**1947**  John William (Jack) Carter is born.

**1948**  Carter is assigned to the submarine USS *Pomfret.*

**1949**  Carter is assigned to the USS *Seawolf.*

**1950**  James Earl (Chip) Carter III is born. North Korea invades South Korea.

**1952**  Carter is promoted to lieutenant. Carter is assigned to the Atomic Energy Commission. Donnel Jeffrey (Jeff) Carter is born.

**1953**  Earl Carter dies in Plains. Carter receives an honorable discharge from the Third Naval District.

**1954**  U.S. Supreme Court ends segregation in public schools with *Brown v. Board of Education.*

**1955**  Blacks in Montgomery, Alabama, boycott segregated bus lines.

**1963**  Carter is sworn in as a Georgia state senator.

**1966**  Carter loses the election for governor of Georgia.

**1967**  Amy Lynn Carter is born.

**1970**  Carter is elected governor of Georgia.

**1976**  Carter is elected president of the United States.

**1978**  The Camp David Accords take place.

**1979** China receives diplomatic recognition. Iran takes U.S. hostages.

**1980** Carter loses the election for a second term as president.

**1982** Carter becomes a Distinguished Professor at Emory University. The Carter Center is established at Emory. Carter works for Habitat for Humanity.

**1983** Lillian Carter dies.

**1986** The Carter Center officially opens.

**1987** A national historic site is created in Plains.

**1989** Carter tries to settle a civil war between Ethiopia and Eritrean rebels.

**1992** The Carter Center's Global 2000 program oversees elections in Ghana.

**1994** Carter meets with the North Korean president to resolve the crisis over the country's nuclear weapons program. Carter negotiates a cease-fire in Sarajevo, Bosnia-Herzegovina, between the Bosnians and Serbs.

**1995** Carter visits the African countries of Sudan and Uganda to help ease conflicts.

**1996** Carter monitors the Palestinian election.

**1997** Carter monitors the presidential election in Liberia.

**2002** Carter visits Fidel Castro in Cuba. Carter is awarded the Nobel Peace Prize.

# SOURCE NOTES

7 Jimmy Carter, "2002 Nobel Peace Lecture: The Complete Text," *The Carter Center,* December 10, 2002. <http://www.cartercenter.org/viewdoc.asp?docID=1233&submenu=news> (July 11, 2003).

7 Jeffrey Gettleman, "Nobel Prize Awarded to Carter, with Jab at Bush," *New York Times,* October 11, 2002, A1.

7 Ibid.

8 Ibid.

8 Ibid.

8 Peter Jennings, *ABC Evening News,* October 12, 2002.

9 Molly Ivins, *San Francisco Chronicle,* October 16, 2002.

9 Frank Bruni, *New York Times,* December 11, 2002.

13 Jimmy Carter, *Why Not the Best?* (Nashville: Broadman Publishers, 1975), 7.

14 Jimmy Carter, *An Hour Before Daylight: Memories of a Rural Boyhood* (New York: Simon and Schuster, 2001), 39.

17 Ibid., 49.

18 Ibid., 229.

19 Ibid., 95.

19 Ibid., 230.

19–20 Ibid.

22 Jimmy Carter, *Why,* 161.

25 Rosalynn Carter, *First Lady from Plains* (Boston: Houghton Mifflin Company, 1984), 161.

26 Ibid., 24.

26 Peter G. Bourne, *Jimmy Carter: A Comprehensive Biography from Plains to Postpresidency (*New York: Scribner, 1997), 52.

26–27 Ibid., 53.

31 Bourne, 64.

33 Ibid., 63.

35 Ibid., 70.

36 Jimmy Carter, *Why,* 64.

37 Ibid., 65.

37 Jimmy Carter, *Hour,* 258.

40 Ibid., 97.

46 Jimmy Carter, *Why,* 96.

47 Ibid., 138.

48 Ibid., 149.

50 Hugh Carter and Frances Spatz Leighton, *Cousin Beedie and Cousin Hot: My Life with the Carter Family of Plains, Georgia* (Englewood Cliffs, NJ: Prentice-Hall, 1978), 117.

51 Ibid., 116.

52 Ibid., 204.

52 Ibid., 200.

53 Rosalynn Carter, 79.

54 Bourne, 205.

54 Carter and Leighton, 129.

54 Bourne, 218.

55 Ibid., 207.

56 Ibid., 217.

57 Jimmy Carter, *Why,* 151.

57 Ibid., 124.

57 Carter and Leighton, 147.

58 Jimmy Carter, *Why,* 119.

61 Bourne, 264.

63 Rosalyn Carter, 137.

64 Bourne, 336.

65 "The Outsider President," *American President.org,* n.d., <http://www.americanpresident.org/kotrain/courses/JC/JC_in__brief.htm> (April 4, 2002).

65 Bourne, 264.

66 Ibid., 338.

66 Rosalynn Carter, 142.

69 Jimmy Carter, *Keeping Faith: Memoirs of a President,* (New York: Bantam Books, 1982), 21–22.

70 Bourne, 384.

70 Ibid., 387.

70 Micah 6:8.

70 Jimmy Carter, *Keeping Faith,* 17.

70 Ibid.

72 Bourne, 366.
76 Douglas Brinkley, *The Unfinished Presidency: Jimmy Carter's Journey Beyond the White House* (New York: Penguin Books, 1998), 402.
76 Martin Gilbert, *Israel: A History* (New York: William Morrow, 1998), 489.
77 Rosalynn Carter, 238.
77 Ibid., 252.
78 Ibid., 253.
78 Jimmy Carter, *Keeping Faith,* 390.
79 Bourne, 410.
80 Jimmy Carter, *Keeping Faith,* 388.
80 Rosalynn Carter, 251.
81 Brinkley, 26.
81 Ibid.
86 Ibid., 456.
87 Rosalynn Carter, 314.
88 Ibid.
88 Jimmy Carter, 2001, interviewed by Charlie Rose, *Charlie Rose,* Public Broadcasting System, December 5.
90 Brinkley, 127.

91 Jimmy Carter, *Keeping Faith,* 4.
92 Brinkley, xi.
92 Ibid., 40.
92 Ibid., 39.
93 Carter and Leighton, 93.
93 Brinkley, 49.
94 Ibid., 95.
94 Ibid., 51.
94 Ibid., 171.
95 Ibid., 63.
95 Ibid., 64.
95 Bourne, 482.
96 Ibid., 91.
97 Need more...Carter Center, <http://www.cartercenter.org>.
98 Brinkley, 460.
99 Ibid., 381.
100 Brinkley, 457.
102 David Gonzalez, "Carter Addresses the Cuban Nation and Urges Reform" *New York Times,* May 15, 2002, A1, A10.
102 Jimmy Carter, *Why,* 78.
103 Bourne, 428.
103 Ibid.

# BIBLIOGRAPHY

**Books**

Bourne, Peter G. *Jimmy Carter: A Comprehensive Biography from Plains to Postpresidency.* New York: Scribner, 1997.

Brinkley, Douglas. *The Unfinished Presidency: Jimmy Carter's Journey Beyond the White House.* New York: Penguin Books, 1998.

Carter, Hugh (with Frances Spatz Leighton). *Cousin Beedie and Cousin Hot: My Life with the Carter Family of Plains, Georgia.* Englewood Cliffs, NJ: Prentice-Hall, 1978.

Carter, Jimmy. *The Blood of Abraham: Insights into the Middle East.* Boston: Houghton Mifflin Company, 1985.

———. *An Hour Before Daylight: Memories of a Rural Boyhood.* New York: Simon and Schuster, 2001.

———. *Keeping Faith: Memoirs of a President.* New York: Bantam Books, 1982.

———. *Talking Peace: A Vision for the Next Generation.* New York: Dutton Children's Books, 1993.

———. *The Virtues of Aging.* New York: Ballantine Books, 1998.

———. *Why Not the Best?* Nashville, TN: Broadman Publishers, 1975.

Carter, Rosalynn. *First Lady from Plains.* Boston: Houghton Mifflin Company, 1984.

Gilbert, Martin. *Israel: A History.* New York: William Morrow & Co. Inc., 1998.


**Websites**

"The Outsider President." *AmericanPresident.org.* n.d. <http://www.americanpresident.org/kotrain/courses/JC/JC_in_brief.htm> (April 4, 2002).

*The Carter Center.* 2002. <http://www.cartercenter.org> (June 17, 2003).

"Jimmy Carter—Nobel Lecture." *Nobel e-Museum.* December 10, 2002. <http://www.nobel.se/peace/laureates/2002/carter-lecture.html> (July 17, 2003).


**News and Media**

*ABC Evening News,* October 12, 2002.

Bruni, Frank, "Carter Accepts Nobel and Gives Message on Iraq." *New York Times.* December, 11, 2002, A1, A12.

Carter, Jimmy. 2001. Interviewed by Charlie Rose. *Charlie Rose.* Public Broadcasting System, December 5.

Carter, Jimmy. 2001. Interviewed by Terry Gross. *Fresh Air.* National Public Radio, December 5.

Gettleman, Jeffrey. "Nobel Peace Prize Awarded to Carter, with Jab at Bush" *New York Times,* December 11, 2002.

Ivins, Molly. "Nobel Gives Prize—Pundit Gives Offense." *San Francisco Chronicle,* October 16, 2002.

Smith, Terence. 2002. "Post Presidential Works of Jimmy Carter." *NewsHour.* Public Broadcasting System, May 15.

# FURTHER READING

Doyle, Kevin. *Submarines.* Minneapolis: Lerner Publishing Company, 2004.

George, Linda, and Charles George. *Jimmy Carter: Builder of Peace.* Chicago: Children's Press, 2000.

Hobkirk, Lori. *James Earl Carter: Our 39th President.* Chanhassen, MN: The Child's World, 2002.

Joseph, Paul. *Jimmy Carter: United States President.* Minneapolis: Abdo and Daughters, 1999.

Katz, Samuel M. *Jerusalem or Death: Palestinian Terrorism.* Minneapolis: Lerner Publishing Company, 2003.

LaDoux, Rita C. *Georgia.* Minneapolis: Lerner Publshing Company, 2002.

Taus-Bolstad, Stacy. *Iran in Pictures.* Minneapolis: Lerner Publishing Company, 2004.

Wade, Linda R. *Encyclopedia of Presidents: James Carter.* Chicago: Childrens Press, 1989.

# INDEX

# ABOUT THE AUTHOR

Beverly Gherman lives in San Francisco, California. She has written biographies about E. B. White, Robert Louis Stevenson, Georgia O'Keeffe, Norman Rockwell, and Ansel Adams.

Her books have been about artists and writers who interpret the world in a unique way. Jimmy Carter is a prolific writer. In his political and historical books, he provides serious, thoughtful concepts. In his personal writing, there is an added tenderness and warmth as he recalls his early years.

She thinks that biographers are like detectives searching for clues. Jimmy Carter left her many clues about his character in the life he has led and in the words he has written.

------------ ✧ ------------

## PHOTO ACKNOWLEDGMENTS

The images in this book are used with the permission of: The White House, pp. 1, 22, 31, 37, 46, 58, 69, 76, 92; Jimmy Carter Library, pp. 2, 12, 14, 17, 18, 20, 21, 26, 27, 28, 30, 42, 48, 49, 53, 54, 55, 60, 68, 71, 72, 74, 78, 81; © Arne Knudsen/Getty Images, p. 6; © Ted Spiegel/CORBIS, p. 10; © Hans Arne Vedlog/All Over Press Norway/Getty Images, p. 11; © CORBIS, pp. 15, 32; Library of Congress, pp. 24 (LC-USZ-62-93508), 33 (LC-USZ-62-70726), 59 (LC-USZ-62-115830); Naval Photographic Center, p. 36; © Kevin Fleming/CORBIS, p. 39; © Bettmann/CORBIS, pp. 41, 43, 75, 85, 87, 89, 90, 94, 96, 97; Boyd Lewis/Atlanta Historical Society, p. 57; © Hulton|Archive by Getty Images, pp. 61, 64, 65; Independent Picture Service, p. 63; Laura Westlund, p. 83; Embassy of the Islamic Republic of Iran, Ottawa, p. 86; © GILBERT LIZ/CORBIS SYGMA, p. 100; © AFP/CORBIS, p. 101.

Front cover: courtesy of the Jimmy Carter Library.